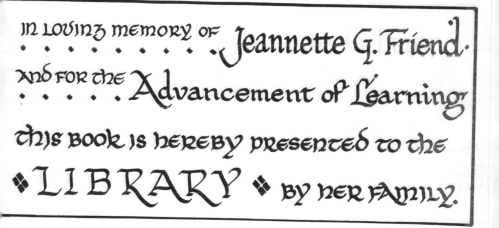

In Loving Memory of Jeannette G. Friend
and for the Advancement of Learning
This Book is Hereby Presented to the
LIBRARY by Her Family.

PERSONAL AND VOCATIONAL INTERPLAY
IN IDENTITY BUILDING:

# PERSONAL AND VOCATIONAL INTERPLAY IN IDENTITY BUILDING

## A LONGITUDINAL STUDY

By JEANNETTE G. FRIEND

Boston
BRANDEN PRESS
Publishers

The author acknowledges permission to quote from the following material:

*On Adolescence* by Peter Blos. Copyright 1962 by The Macmillan Company.

*Normality and Pathology in Childhood* by Anna Freud. Copyright, 1959, by International Universities Press, Inc.

*Identity and the Life Cycle* by Erik H. Erikson. Copyright, 1959, by International Universities Press, Inc.

## ACKNOWLEDGMENTS

It is difficult to convey adequately my genuine gratitude to the many individuals who helped with this book. I want, above all, to express thanks, affection, and respect to the subjects who so patiently and conscientiously shared some of their experiences, opinions, and feelings, as did parents of the younger subjects.

David V. Tiedeman, Professor of Education at Harvard Graduate School of Education, has been a participant from start to finish. In his role of instigator, consultant, and morale builder, he served as the mainspring of the functioning of the group.

Funding and sponsorship came from the New England School Development Council (NESDEC), a nonprofit association of school superintendents. Drs. Donald P. Mitchell, Executive Secretary and his successor, Richard Goodman, deserve special mention for their helpfulness. The Advisory Committee on Research in Guidance accepted responsibility for recommending that the project receive financial support.

To Dr. Douglas P. Dillenbeck of the College Entrance Examination Board goes my sincere appreciation for two generous grants and help with the manuscript.

Dr. Sylvia Korstvedt, Dr. John Arsenian, and Dr. Jeanne Griffen, highly competent psychologists, performed most of the second projective test comparisons. Drs. Sylvia and Arne Korstvedt formulated the Prediction Study.

Dr. Arthur Couch of Harvard University gave wise and sound advice about design. Elizabeth Anderson, Natalie Levin, and Joan Leibovich abstracted some of the case histories to lighten my task. Rita Friend and Carol Rumple contributed competent and conscientious typing service. Friends and colleagues too numerous to mention listened patiently and reacted constructively. My husband, Gerald, helped with record-keeping and with many details. Dr. Esther Mathews worked as co-investigator until she accepted an appointment in the West.

Erik H. Erikson has kindly acknowledged my use of his basic works in this project.

# CONTENTS

PART III — THE WOMEN'S LIBERATION MOVEMENT

# FOREWORD

Among the critical issues confronting educators today those that cluster around the area of identity formation and ego building and those that are related to career development are central. How to help individuals build personally satisfying and responsible life styles at a time when they are being threatened by unprecedented forces of change and upheaval in organizational structures and occupational relationships presents one of the most persistent challenges of our times. The author of this study has made a significant and unique contribution to an understanding of the positive and negative forces and factors in identity building and career development and the interpenetration of these aspects of personal growth and occupational experience.

The book is distinctive for the substantial research effort that has been invested in its production. It presents a highly responsible and rarely undertaken longitudinal study of human development which incorporates histories of girls and women to provide in-depth information, insights and developmental progress reports of four groups each comprising ten persons at the pre-adolescent, mid-adolescent, young adult and generative stages of growth. The impressive case history data, gathered over a period of years by highly qualified researchers and consultants, are interpreted according to the stages of identity formation postulated by Erik Erikson which give admirable cohesion to the study and furnishes practitioners with a foundation of personality theory for understanding individual, group and vocational behavior observed in daily practice.

Although the study is confined to histories of girls and women it is not narrow because of this. Rather, in revealing information on their views, values and experiences and the impact of these on changing roles and relationships, the data provided are rewardingly rich in detail on kinds of factors contributing to behavior modification that cut across sex, age, cultural and social differences.

This study will be of special value to counselors and counselor educators but can be read with profit by parents, teachers, administrators, social workers and others in helping roles. In successive case presentations the author draws on an analysis and synthesis of forty interviews, school reports and projective tests to interpret behavior and to suggest kinds of interventions that could make a difference in the coping ability of individuals to solve particular problems and do more effective planning.

Beyond the data that sometimes speak of personal suffering from a sense of lack of community and loss-of-self are the fruits of the author's findings that throw more light on how individual girls and women may transcend the threats of an impersonal society, affirm her being, provide for personal liberation, and become an agent of her own adjustment and self-actualization.

J. WENDELL YEO, PH.D.
*Professor of Education*
*Boston University*

# INTRODUCTION

When Alice in Wonderland asked, "Would you tell me, please, which way I ought to go from here?", the Cheshire Cat replied, "That depends a good deal on where you want to get to." This is the dominant theme of what follows. For there are multiple ways of life, not only a single path; there are highways, byways, brooks, and trails to follow if our goals are clear. Some are well-trodden paths, others dense with thickets; the latter attract the trailblazers. Like Robert Frost, a few prefer the road "less travelled by."

In the early 1960's I set out to explore and examine the concept of identity formation in the context of occupational roles for girls and women. These two developmental areas differed substantially in the lives of men and women — a discrepancy which has biological or built-in psychological, social or cultural roots. The investigation encompasses the lives of a total of forty girls and women at different age and developmental levels. Because of space limitations I can present only a small portion of their histories here. The lives of the total sample — their hopes and aspirations, triumphs and disappointments, attachments and avoidances, convictions and attitudes toward self — were traced and fully examined, but my interest was especially focused on the subjects' choices, as regards life-style and occupation. Moreover I watched the younger girls develop and grow up occupationally.

The age and grade levels at which the histories were studied correspond to the stages in identity formation postulated by Erik Erikson. For example, the sixth-grade girls were age 11 and in the stage of what Erikson calls "industry" at the positive pole, with its counterpart of inferiority at the negative one. (These

[11]

stages are described in more detail in Chapter 2; they are at the hub of the book.)

There was considerable gain from the scheduled talks with each parent — talks which conveyed the climate of the home, and the subtle interactions which might have affected the parents' identities.

Erikson suggests (in *Childhood and Society*, 1963): "The autobiographies of extraordinary (and extraordinarily self-perceptive) individuals are a suggestive source of insight into the development of identity. In order to find an anchor point for the discussion of the universal genetics of identity, however, it would be well to trace its development through significant life episodes of 'ordinary' individuals."

The girls and women in this book are such ordinary individuals, persons of middle-middle class socio-economic backgrounds, living in the suburbs of a city. They want to be, or have become, wives, mothers, teachers, nurses, dietitians, scientists, social workers, buyers, dance critics, technical and fiction writers, fashion coordinators or lawyers. The manner in which they came to choose their goals is, as Erikson suggests, one source of insight into growth of identity, and also one of the chief preoccupations of this book. Through Erikson's work, the term "identity" has acquired new richness and complexity of meaning. Identity denotes sameness and continuity; something enduring yet changing, a sense of me-ness and we-ness. There are personal identities, family and group; masculine and feminine; borrowed ones and others which are noted for their authenticity in sense of self. Through our identities, we express ourselves, our beliefs, strivings, roles and goals. Of particular interest are sex identities and vocational goals.

The word "identity" now crowds the mass media; the conversations of college students, teenagers, and more sophisticated adults. "I don't know who I am," they complain. Few can define identity or name the ingredients which form its texture

[12]

and quality. Erikson has contributed a wealth of data, especially in tracing the eight stages of ego development which furnish researchers with valuable guide posts. (See Chapter 2.) One of the fundamental issues in the infancy stage is a basic sense of trust versus mistrust. Whether it develops positively or negatively hinges on the mother's sensitive, dependable, rhythmic response to her babies' needs. Sameness and regularity are all important to the infant as is the quality of the emotional relationship between mother and child.

I have taken an especially close look at the early adolescent years, and the mid-adolescent and late adolescent stages, for these are periods when identity as it relates to the choice of an occupation and way of life should take on discernible structure. At the outset the sixth graders were pre-adolescents at age eleven; on returning three years later, they had reached the stage of early adolescence. I have also sampled women in young adulthood or post-adolescence; some in the generative stage and a few in the stage of integrity versus despair. The high school seniors formerly in the stage of mid-adolescence were now in the late phase of this period and usually at college when they returned for a second work up.

The central significance of a wise choice of occupation and life pattern is eloquently stated by Bruno Bettelheim in *The Informed Heart,* the poignant story of his concentration camp experience. "It is my conviction, he writes, "that to withstand and counteract the deadening impact of mass society, of emphasis on technical progress rather than human progress, or domination by machines and mass media, a man's work must be permeated with his personality, should reflect *his own purpose in life* and not mere convenience, chance, or expediency; but should directly reflect how he reaches for self realization in this world."

The problem of self-realization is even more complex for women. Marian K. Sanders, writing in *Harper's* Magazine, referred to the status of women as a problem which has reached

[13]

crisis proportions comparable to air pollution and urban sprawl. For women face special interruptions of work — periods for the bearing and caring of children. They do not usually resume work until the children are ready for school or until they leave home for college. When husbands are transferred to different sections of the country, there may or may not be opportunities for their wives to return to their previous occupations. But when wives are reassigned, their husbands rarely accompany them because the husband's income is usually larger.

Often women are plagued with doubt as to whether or not to pursue a career which they really want, or to compromise with a convenient setting and work hours. Or they exclude work from their lives altogether. The social climate in which many have grown up frowns on an occupation outside of the home after marriage and on continuing education beyond that which will ensure capability for earning a living.

Some husbands still object to working wives, while a diminishing number of women are truly content at home. Women who may be especially creative within the home often feel second rate there, particularly after exposure to the current mass media.

This book's aim is an ambient one; it leads directly to the counselor's goal of assisting the student in her search for identity and for self insight. But educators must help in providing the counselor with an armamentarium of viable concepts as well as expertise in implementing them. At the heart of the book, are the developmental concepts defined by Erikson. He states in his chapter of Blaine and MacArthur's book *(Emotional Problems of the Student,* 1961) that the tasks of each growth stage should be fulfilled at the very stage of its emergence; and that a tentative decision should be made by the counselor or preferably by a team as to whether the adolescent's dilemma is diffuse and fleeting on the one hand, or durable and more sustained as well as of greater severity on the other. The cumulative aspect of the school record furnishes a valuable perspective in this decision.

[14]

The case histories have been cast at a deeper-than-usual level to elicit the psychodynamic aspects of vocational choices as well as for the teaching of counseling. They offer a body of data which is expensive to collect and even more costly to analyze and distill. In many histories twenty-five hours were needed to digest and amalgamate these data. But they were rewarding and effective in illustrating the growth of identity and some of the meanings of choices of occupations. For the dynamics between identity and vocation stands out and reveals partially what is going on in the work situation. Why, for instance does the worker get along well with a young foreman and not with an older man? Clearly this situation seems to reflect the universal experience of the *repetition compulsion,* a mechanism often used in understanding psychological data but rarely seen in the counseling literature. In the work setting, the employee reacts to the older supervisor or foreman as he did in his earlier experiences with a particularly domineering father who caused the worker considerable anxiety which seemed to carry over to his work relationships as well as functioning — both important mechanisms in adjusting and progressing on the job. Such reactions take place more clearly with attitudes towards the same sex parent, and may have overtones emanating from the earlier triangular situation in the family structure.

Another mechanism with widespread counseling implications but still used both rarely and loosely is that of *sublimation.* An example is the man whose mother was overambitious for him and concentrated her efforts on arranging training for the academic and/or professional success which her businessman husband lacked. As might be expected, this man's personality developed large components of feminine identity which he learned to *sublimate* through identifying with children and becoming a talented teacher after continued failure in the early grades.

In addition to the central thesis, there are a number of ancillary ones: the special dilemmas of women who work as well as stay at home; the quickening of the interaction tempo when girls around the age of 14 meet with peer groups for a free-wheeling discussion of their future life style.

The core concept of the book embraces a number of themes. Their rationale in tracing the interplay between personal and vocational behavior serves to build the ego maximally by drawing on these two areas instead of only one. Added strength can be derived from these dual sources of identity — a double portion.

Identification is a third way of communicating; it is expanded in Chapter 2, "Identifications." Some women will find their identity and major gratification in being with their children until school age; others in continuing in their special field of work, together with caring for home and children, and in social pursuits or renewed interest in former hobbies. There is a dearth of material in the literature dealing with girls and women in this perspective. I felt the need for a fresh and more complete grasp, empirically derived, of occupational choice phenomena and practice.

The stance selected is one in which I could view the process of choice in individual histories *as it was happening and becoming* in the pre-adolescents. This gives a quality of immediacy and vividness to the material. I brought to it the conviction that the individual is both agent and reactor, that to varying degrees she writes her own biography within the limits of her unique biological and experiential background.

It is my belief that occupation can be a resource for enriching personality, more especially that part which we think of as identity, the images of self, beliefs, tasks, aspirations that are peculiarly one's own. These in turn influence the choice of an occupation. Identity formation is the inner phenomenon, the integration of a long series of identifications; choice of occupational role is an outer expression of identity; yet these two

[16]

phenomena dovetail. I have looked at both of these aspects of the subjects' lives as well as the interaction between them. It is a vantage point, I think, which presents a meaningful, organized perspective to those charged with counseling and counselor education. Yet I could find no mention of the repetition compulsion in the counseling literature. "We have all experienced the occasional need of talking incessantly about a painful event which one might be expected to want to forget. We also suspect that it is not so innocently accidental that some people make the same mistakes over and over again — to marry the same kind of partner, for instance. . . "(Erikson, 1963) The need to reenact painful experiences verbally or through action in an effort to allay anxiety (the repetition compulsion) is found also in repetitive dreams or play contained in but a single theme or other duplicating behavior. In constant job changing and dissatisfaction especially, one sees a worker who seems to look for and meet the very upsetting situation which he has spent almost a lifetime trying to conquer. He seems drawn toward the overauthoritative boss, who is even violent at times. The worker seems to "ask for" angry reactions which he could not earlier tolerate in his father. But if he could succeed in breaking the chain of repetition, he might have a device of adaptation instead of neurosis. Here is the heart of why the selection of an occupational role is so critical, as is some grasp of the structure and practice of the work environment in meeting the needs of the individual employee. If possible the counselor needs some awareness of the personnel practices of individual plants in the community.

The Prediction Study (see Appendix) provided an additional device for learning from the subjects. After the first contact with the high school seniors in 1963, I made tentative statements about the changes I would expect three years later. Errors, I anticipated, might be fruitful learning experiences whereas the more accurate predictions would serve in some measure as

[17]

validation for some of the conceptual formulations on which they were based. This is reported in the chapter on predictions.

These analyses have added up to a book consisting of seven rather than forty available life histories. The total number of histories has been used in the calculation of percentages in reporting the clinical characteristics of each group of subjects. The analyses and speculations will, I expect, lead to conclusions meaningful to counselors by specifying how these factors relate to identity formation and occupational role. Such data have relevance for those who are interested in fields related to counseling, in schools, colleges, and industry, and social agencies; also for parents, in discussing occupations with the children; with school administrators, and teachers who are important role models, frequently playing the counselor's part. Chapter 13 will develop its application to the practice and teaching of counseling.

I am aware of the research limitations of the small number of cases in each group; the uniform social class of the first two groups which make extrapolation especially applicable to middle-middle class groups in a suburban school setting with high level academic standards. Though I have accumulated stacks of data on the subjects, I am also aware that the term "life history" is somewhat presumptuous, for I recognize my limitations in penetrating the mysteries and complexities of another's life.

Erikson's ideas constitute the fulcrum of this book. I have the highest respect and admiration for his work which has enlarged appreciably my own knowledge of human behavior. His name has become almost a household word, his theories have world-wide renown. According to the Erikson system, one does not give up with the five-year-old patient who is still having difficulty; instead, the therapist counts on a reorganization and upsurge of integration and consolidation in the industry and late-adolescent stages. In my approach, I look to the job situation, too, as a source of this, and have faith that the gratification

[18]

emanating from work can partially absorb the individual's emotional pressures if they are customed to fit.

Erikson's interest in the work situation is rare among psychoanalysts. He uses words with a business connotation such as "accrued," while work, he says, is the backbone of identity. Moreover an entire period of the life cycle is devoted to growth in the industry stage around age eleven. But he does not stop at the door of occupation; he goes on to include in his theories other phases of living; childhood, love, the middle years, aging, and death.

It is this sensible and sensitive concern with the realities as well as the reveries of life which alerted me to the possible value of adapting parts of his system to the field of counseling.

As a generic term, adolescence is the stage when the task is to start on the crystallization of occupational and life style. But the breakdown which Blos has made into five substages of adolescence makes the process of counseling more precise. A young adolescent, age 14, is quite a different girl from the mid-adolescent at from 16 to 18. In addition to this refinement of terms, Erikson's "Eight Stages of Man" provides a framework highlighting the emergence and progression from stage to stage, step by step, each depending on the resolution of the previous one. After presenting the stages and the tasks of each, I will examine some of the progress as well as the lag.

# PART I

## Introductory Discussion

# CHAPTER 1
## Theory and Methods

My goal is to learn more about how girls grow up occupationally — how they respond to their environmental soil and climate, and deal with interpersonal relations in the family, in school, and in work. I am especially interested in the identifications which result and influence choice of a work role; and the process by which identifications merge into a variety of identities. While the fields of counseling and guidance are enriched by highly competent, even brilliant theorists, little has resulted in the way of available and useful theory as Tiedeman and Guinzberg have so often said.

The formulations of White, Tiedeman, Roe, Mathewson, Borow, Arbuckle, and Hartman to mention a few, suggest an awareness of the mutuality and reciprocity between the personal identity and job horizons. Most, however, do not go further in search of forces which forge the connecting link between person and work. Super has skillfully developed the self concept as a key tool. Even more generally, there has been sparse investigation of the harnessing of the energy generated by the occupation, its nature and potential for gratification. Yet we all know individuals whose sense of self has been nourished by experiencing group solidarity, and other gratifications inherent in the job.

There are multiple connotations to Erikson's use of the term "identity." He writes in his *Childhood and Society* (1959): "At one time, then, it will appear to be a conscious sense of individual identity; at another to be an unconscious striving for a *continuity* of personal character; at a third, as a criterion for the silent doings of ego *synthesis;* and finally as a maintenance of an inner solidarity with a group's ideals and identity. . . ."

[23]

*"Identity formation,"* he continues, "emerges as an evolving configuration — a configuration which is gradually established by successive ego syntheses and resyntheses throughout childhood; it is a configuration gradually integrating constitutional givens, idiosyncratic libidinal needs, favored capacities, significant identifications, effective defenses, successful sublimations, and consistent roles. . . . Achievement of this synthesis is the aspiration of every person who must make an occupational decision."

The work of Blos contributes to a deep and dynamic grasp of the various stages *within* adolescence in his excellent book called *On Adolescence* (1962). He has refined the generic concept of adolescence, breaking it down into five parts or stages and elaborating each. We see clearly the difference between a pre-adolescent and an early adolescent. Moreover, Blos translates these into ego values that relate directly to occupational ones. And he describes in detail the normal development of girls as contrasted with boys. More than this, he states the operating principle used to synthesize his data.

In Blos' search for this operating principle explaining what takes place in late adolescence, he discusses the spurts of growth and consolidation which accelerate ego synthesis. This does not mean that all of the vestiges of unresolved trauma or conflicts, which are universal phenomena in childhood, vanish. Rather they are made more specific and ego syntonic. Girls in this stage acquire a grip on what they will be like as adults and this often enhances self-esteem. There is a staking out of life spaces, and work comes into sharper focus.

Blos continues, "Through the emotional transformation which affords greater purpose and direction . . . the consolidation process in late adolescence wields a selective affinity for certain choices. In addition they furnish a relentless force which propels the growing subject toward a certain way of life which he comes to feel is his very own. The force is generated by the *repetition compulsion* or urge to master which pushes unintegrated experi-

[24]

ences into mental life for eventual mastery now that the ego is stronger. Rather than asking 'who am I' the late adolescent is apt to say 'this is me.' "

Erikson (in "Problems of Ego Identity," *Psychological Issues,* 1953) sees identity formation beginning where the usefulness of identification ends. "It arises from the selective repudiation and mutual assimilation of childhood identifications and their absorption in a new configuration, which, in time, is dependent on the process by which a society (often through sub-societies) identifies the young individual, recognizing him as someone who had to become the way he is, and who, being the way he is, is taken for granted." Identity formation, Erikson feels, neither begins or ends with adolescence. It is a life-long development, largely unconscious, to the individual and his society.

Some of the roots of the conflict in women's identities and its relation to occupational role are suggested here. Our society views identity in men and women basically in sex roles. In men it is generally enhanced and strengthened by occupation; in women, on the other hand, sex role is sometimes confused by occupational role if it be other than family. Perhaps society backs this situation in order to protect and insure the biological functioning of women. Identity unfolds through the mother, especially if she recognizes and meets the special needs of the child.

White in *Lives in Progress* (1966) writes cogently of the vital importance of vocational choice in our American culture. The latter imposes a role which permeates one's life. He believes that other aspects — such as status, power, reward for achievement — are significant, and that a wise choice promotes growth. His concepts of competence and effectance motivation are indeed useful in counseling.

*Formulation of internalization and definition of terms*

A network of psychic mechanisms are central to all choices, but especially to that of career. One of these mechanisms is the

[25]

overall process of internalization — a pervasive pattern which epitomizes transformation of external to internal. The superego system illustrates this phenomenon.

Internalization is the umbrella or overall concept but there are auxiliary break-downs for readers who want to go into the theory more thoroughly. From this viewpoint *identification* is a key and complex ego function which has both defensive and developmental or adaptive features, with which I will be primarily concerned. Identification is a way of achieving through habitual *imitative* activities, various degrees of modeling of one's personality in the image of another person, or part of the whole person. This image is soaked in or internalized so that it is continually present whether or not the actual model is. The individual wants to increase her resemblance to this model. Defensive identification, on the other hand, is close to incorporation but connotes primary process or more primitive thinking.

There are also refinements or auxiliary functions which I will merely enumerate here. These include what Schafer *(Aspects of Internalization,* 1970) calls self and object representations or images. The former usually pertains to the individual's own body and personality, while the object representations are always involved in feelings and attitudes toward other people. The auxiliary mechanisms also include *learning, fantasy,* and *imitation.*

One can clearly grasp how a positive identification with father spurs the learning process and firms the conscience. The fact that father learns and the subject wants to resemble him is at the core of the dynamics.

I use the term *ego* in Erikson's (1963) sense. He defines it as "a selective, integrative, coherent, and persistent agency central to personality formation," the inner "organ" which makes it possible for man to bind together the two great evolutionary development, *his inner life and his social planning.*

*Identity* is unique to the individual; it is not static. Rather it emerges and changes throughout the life span. Deriving pri-

[26]

marily from the integration of identifications, and consisting of the strivings, goals, hopes, and values with which the individual views herself and what she stands for, it is a sense of "me-ness." Parsons *(The Social System,* 1951) views this as partially but not exclusively internalization. In learning to live with her family the young child internalizes her thoughts, feelings, actions, and values of culture. But Erikson *(ibid)* has also added and clarified the concept which stands for the social framework enfolding the individual. There have been accusations that Erikson has forgotten the unconscious; this is not justified. Although the young child's identity usually buds fairly early, it is not until adolescence (mid or late) that it takes more durable shape.

*Social class:* The Hollingshead Scale is derived from the Index of Social Position developed by Hollingshead and Redlich (1955). This index is based on factors of residence, occupation and education rated on a seven-point scale and multiplied by a factor weight determined by a regression equation.

*Occupation:* I am using the term in the generic sense to include whatever occupies the individual, be it care of the home, children, companionship with husband, club work, politics, church work, pursuit of hobbies or career.

*Repetition compulsion* exemplifies a universal reenactment of the worker's effort to conquer and control early anxiety over conflicts with a domineering father, now reactivated and reenacted in the current work setting and often resulting in friction with the boss. "He reminds me of my father who wanted to run my life," the worker often complains.

*Methodology and procedures*

The overall approach to the ordering of these data include the ideographic, or individual case study, and the nomothetic, or study of each group at each stage of development: pre-adolescence, young adolescence, mid-adolescence, late and post-adolescence. The study is in a process-outcome design, aimed at developing formulations if not theory.

Tiedeman states (in *Harvard Studies in Career Development*): "What is needed in guidance is a reintegration of the conceptualizing of its task around a theory of personality development." Backed by our parallel convictions, I chose the life history, however difficult, as my method, because my conception of personality emphasizes its changing or dynamic nature and the course it takes in a *configuration* of thoughts, feelings and behavior functioning in a social milieu. Such a conception is held by many but has been systematized primarily by Murray (1963) and White (1963). It calls for the studying of lives as wholes and certainly over a period of time.

How to process the material while maintaining the wholeness of the individual presented a knotty problem. Dr. Arthur Couch, Associate Professor of Psychology at Harvard and a leader in the statistical analysis of clinical material, felt that correlational methods were inappropriate because of the small number of cases in each group, and favored instead the use of case histories which were attuned to the stage approach. The number of informants, the varying sources from which inferences were drawn, and the Prediction Study all contribute a respectable degree of reliability and validity.

Interpenetration of identity with occupational role holds the potential for knitting together the elements of the ego into a sense of unity and wholeness — a goal sought by all of us. Not only does it contribute to continuity basic to the sense of being an ordered part of a vaster, meaningful whole, it supplies balm to the inner self.

The twenty younger subjects, ten in the sixth and ten in the twelfth grades, were interviewed and tested at two intervals over a three-year period. The cascade feature of the design — using subjects at successive age levels — allowed me to view them in time perspective, with the girls in the first two groups approxi-

[28]

mating "younger sister" status in comparison with the older subjects in Groups III and IV — a simulated longitudinal design. But in addition, I used an *actual* longitudinal plan of studying subjects at two intervals three years apart. By seeing the girls at ages 14, 17, 20, and 26, we have spanned adolescence in its early, middle and late periods. Since adolescence is the stage when the developmental task consists of crystallizing and consolidating an identity and a decision, however tentative, of an occupational area, I have a broad view of this important time in the lives of the girls *as it is happening.* Toward its end, I see evidence in some girls of an effort towards consolidation and integration, as well as a higher degree of competence in interpersonal relations.

The girls in Groups I and II were students in a suburban public school system with an excellent reputation; those in Group III were 1957 graduates of either an eastern "Seven Sisters" college or of a large urban university. Group I girls were selected by the principal of their primary school according to the criteria mentioned above, with the added stipulation that they must be age eleven since we wanted prepubertal girls. Group II girls were seniors at the local high school and were opted by counselors from those who expressed willingness to participate and whose parents also agreed. Another stipulation was that they had visited the guidance office within a designated period.

Their college class president selected the Group III women according to the criteria of marital status, stage of development, and reactions to work. Availability also was a screening device. Members of Group III were selected because they added to the range, and were willing to participate plus representing a group in the generative stage.

*The Group Meeting*

I met once in a group with the girls in Group I, the pre-adolescents originally, now in early adolescence and age 14. *Its purpose*

[29]

*was to offset their current inertness.* Both individual interviews and test responses were quite barren; fantasy stories were concerned with loss of parents. Blatant apathy and depression were characteristic; it was hard to recall the ebullience and vibrance of these same subjects when they were 11. Fourteen is an age when many girls form strong attachments to other girls. I thought, therefore, that a group meeting might be more productive and this proved to be true. Individuals seemed to be supported by the group, adding spontaneity and lively, informative participation.

What seemed to intrigue this group at 14 was a current incident resulting in the suspension of a classmate whom they accused of being sexually promiscuous. The girls exchanged bits of knowledge of many fascinating episodes, and seemed to vie with each other as to who had the choicest morsel. Some were sympathetic, blaming the student's plight on friends or family difficulties; others condemned her. Half thought she could be helped by seeing the school psychiatrist, a few thought she didn't want to change. The conformers lined up against the rebels.

Nor could we find anything in the literature written in depth, and studying girls and women over time with focus on occupation. Yet we all know individuals whose identities have flourished when fed by the experience of group solidarity at work, or by virtue of the actual gratifications work offers — gratifications meaningful because they are germane to the personal identity of the worker. The social interaction with fellow workers, the personalities of the leaders, their degree of appreciation for a job well done, the remuneration and other forms of security — to mention a few — all are among the possible rewards.

A multi-pronged approach appears to characterize the huge and complex field of vocational choice and work relevant behavior, again both universals. Many people are quick to ask what a person works at and how he came to select it; they seem intrigued with this life dilemma.

[30]

The role of the worker — one which consumes scores of days months and years — also shapes social, socio-economic, and to some extent the workers' marital life, the nature of friendships and a large segment of their general values. The situational aspects of the job are particularly important — the kind of supervisor and fellow worker and the sensitivity of the overall emotional climate of the plant. In America, especially, occupation is one of the chief sources of identity. When asked at a social gathering, "Who is he?" the reply is usually given in terms of career (an architect or a sales manager), whereas in European countries, family and residence might be emphasized instead.

*Vocation seems to be a key to the door of identity.* The reverse also holds and the combination can spring the lock. It was partially for this reason that we have in Part III introduced the psycho-social and vocational aspects of the Women's Liberation movement whose members appear to differ sharply from those of the young adults — a comparison group which emphasizes the potential gratifications emanating from self realization and other job satisfactions influencing life style.

Other writers in this field branch out and focus on such important facets as work adjustment and the importance of the climate of the work situation as well as its manipulation by the counselor or personnel man within the individual plant where the worker is employed. Neff *(Work and Behavior,* 1969), who is searching for a theory of work adjustment, believes that such values as self-esteem and the restoration of confidence are especially significant.

[31]

# CHAPTER 2
## The Research Materials

*The Erikson stages of ego development*

Since the Erikson stages offer a framework for studying the subjects, I have borrowed and used them as guidelines; the rendering is mine. A brilliant psychoanalyst, psychologist, and anthropologist, Erikson emphasizes the ego's synthesizing function. He sees his book *Childhood and Society* as a psychoanalytic study of the relation of the ego to society, a relationship in which the individual constantly develops in personality. The polarities — positive and negative — struggle for dominance. In the early stages both gratifications and conflict center on the mother, for the infant's first and most strategic task is to develop trust — trust in herself, and in her mother — both accompanied by a sense of well-being. Because she both loves and resents her mother, ambivalence runs rampant. The mouth is the main focus of pleasure. This stage corresponds to the psychoanalytic oral one, and usually extends through the first year. The quality of development comes about through interaction with her mother.

But struggles do often arise between mother and child around the age of eighteen months when a new sibling may arrive or when there is a thrust of autonomy versus shame and doubt, battles over toilet training in the second or anal stage. The latter mirrors the toddler's psychological dependence and still limited body growth, her urges to assert herself on the one hand and doubt of her ability on the other. The child loves her mother, but she is also angry with her for the restrictions which mother needs to impose. Autonomy is a critical stage for the development of will and control of impulse.

The stage of initiative versus guilt is marked by signs of beginning sex role formation. Now the father tends to upstage the mother. The triangular situation has considerable impact, and the child's identification with the mother becomes still more ambivalent. Activities and fantasies abound. Now she has learned to manage muscles and words quite well. Erikson calls this the stage of initiative on the one hand and guilt on the other. It corresponds to the phallic or urethral stage when the boy becomes intrusive in his activity while the girl takes a more receptive position, and tends to relate with a seductive touch; whereas the boy at this stage has a sense of being "on the make," a phallic, obtrusive mode, the girl tends toward modes of "catching" and "snatching" or in the milder forms of making herself attractive and endearing.

The child has an increased need for exercising her ability, using initiative when exploring on her bike or climbing trees or manipulating complicated toys. She wants to be big, has fantasies of being a giant or a tiger while actually running from them in a panic-like retreat. The failure in actually achieving power arouses guilt, as do the child's rage and disappointment when her efforts at using initiative are quashed and treated as unimportant. The child's fantasies are sexually tinged and this too arouses guilt and castration fears on the basis of the incest taboo. The guilt stimulates overmanipulation of self and a harsh superego.

The industry versus inferiority period covers a longer span, approximately ages 7 to 11. Now the child tends to identify with the same sex parent. The little girl enjoys working on projects with others, cooking and sewing. If she meets with some success and is recognized for her competence, she beams with a sense of accomplishment. But if the tasks are beyond her, and no recognition is given for what she is able to do, she loses her confidence. Fortunately, this work is part of school activities, and separated from the home where inferiority is apt to be the setting of failure. Beginning tasks are introduced at this period

[33]

as a yardstick for measuring progress and other work related ventures.

The identity stage is at times referred to as the identity crisis, and is a critical one. Failure to establish a firm identity, yet one subject to change, leads to role diffusion and to a sense of alienation. Hers is the current task of coming to grips with the family romance which is reactivated at this time, as well as with a sense of self. With the former task, she uses the tactic of finding a boy friend around her own age. The girl's ego becomes stronger; she is more capable in the abstract realm of knowledge, and can empathize with people. These help her perform the synthesizing function of the ego, and build wholes out of parts. Thus she is able to both understand and to relate to people.

The sixth stage is that of the young adult — a period of court-ship and early family life and/or of professional progress. Erik-son includes more than the physical intimacy. (He calls the stage intimacy versus isolation.) For those who lack a man in their lives, work and friends substitute. The task here is to grow psychologically through motherhood and wifehood or work. Sometimes the husband fears being overwhelmed or swallowed up in the intimacy, and while this bodes ill, it need not be a permanent failure.

Generativity versus self-absorption relates to the middle years. It is the time when the woman cares genuinely for others, not necessarily relatives. At this period, women are expected to be altruistic and sincerely concerned with the plight of others.

The last stage is called integrity versus despair. The individual is now old; she has time for reflection, and to enjoy grand-children; also for nature if so inclined. Integrity grows out of the individual's ability to look back over life with pleasure and some pride, rather than concentrating on mistakes and what [she] might have done. For she feels it is too late to try again. Rather the person at the positive end of the scale "accepts the idea of one's one and only life cycle and of the people who have

[34]

become significant in it as something that had to be and that by necessity permitted of no substitutions. . . ." On the other hand, loss of this accrued integration *is signified by despair*.

Psychosocial identity, writes Erikson, develops out of a gradual integration of all identifications. But here, if anywhere, the whole has a different quality from the sum of its parts. Under favorable circumstances children have the nucleus of a separate identity early in life; often they must defend it even against the necessity of over-identifying with one or both of their parents. These processes are difficult to study in patients because the neurotic self has, by definition, fallen prey to over-identifications which isolate the young individual both from his budding identity and from his milieu.

Enlarging on the concept of identity, Erikson states that the "danger of role diffusion [the stage at the opposite pole on the Erikson chart] is based on strong previous doubt as to one's sexual identity and can result in delinquency and outright psychotic episodes." He also says, "Cases of severe identity diffusion suffer also from an acute upset in the sense of workmanship and this whether in the form of inability to concentrate or in a self-destructive preoccupation with some one-sided activity."

In most instances, however, it is the inability to settle on an occupational identity which disturbs young people. To keep themselves together, they temporarily over-identify to the extent of apparent loss of their own self. The sense of identity carries with it concern for how to connect the roles and skills cultivated earlier with the occupational prototypes of the day. It is the accrued experience of the ego's ability to integrate all identifications with the vicissitudes of the libido, with the aptitudes developed out of endowment, and with the opportunities offered in social roles. "The sense of identity then, is the accrued confidence that the inner sameness and continuity prepared in the past are matched by the sameness and continuity of one's meaning for others as evidenced in the tangible promise of a career. . . ." To

[35]

repeat, a lasting ego identity cannot begin to exist without the trust of the first oral stage. Each stage comes to its ascendence, meets its crises, and finds its solution during the stage indicated.

*Relation of play to work*

Interpersonal relations play an important part in identity building. The identity does not simply arrive; it evolves from experiences, involvement and commitment to others. The infant for a short period perceives the mother as part of herself. Gradually she becomes aware that her mother is a separate individual, but she is still seen as the source of satisfactions — food, warmth, physical comfort, response. The discovery that there are others in the world gives her an embryonic notion of self. Moreover the benevolent mother also becomes the chief source of frustration and deprivation.

Erikson writes: "The playing child advances forward to new stages of mastery . . . the infantile form of the human ability to deal with experience by creating model situations and to master reality by experiment and planning. . . . The small world of manageable toys is a harbor which the child establishes to return to when she needs to overhaul her ego. . . ." *(Childhood and Society,* 1963).

Anna Freud, in *Normality and Pathology in Childhood* (1965), traces interesting developmental lines, two of which are "From the Body to the Toy and from Play to Work":

1) Play begins with the infant as an activity yielding erotic pleasure involving the mouth, surface of the skin. It is carried out on the child's own body or on the mother's with no clear distinction between the two.

2) The properties of the mother's and the child's body are transferred to some soft substance — a blanket or rug.

3) Clinging to one specific transitional object (blanket) develops further into a more indiscriminating liking for soft toys which are alternately cuddled and mistreated. Toys cannot retaliate for the latter, so that the toddler can express the full range of his ambiv-

[36]

alence toward them. . . . They gradually fade out except for use at bedtime. [Winnicut, in his article, "Transitional Objects and Transitional Phenomena," 1953, has written profoundly on the subject of the transitional object.]

4) Ability to play changes into ability to work when additional faculties are acquired.

a) To control, inhibit, or modify the impulses to use given materials aggressively and destructively, treating them positively and constructively instead.

b) To carry out preconceived plans with a minimum regard for the lack of immediate pleasure yield, intervening frustrations and the maximum regard for the pleasure in the ultimate outcome.

c) To achieve thereby not only the transition from the primitive and instinctual to sublimated pleasure, together with a high grade of *neutralization of the energy employed* but equally the transition from the pleasure to the reality principle in the ultimate, a development which is essential for success in work during latency, adolescence, and in maturity. Day-dreaming, games and hobbies are allied activities significant for ego development.

In general the girls preferred stuffed animals to doll play. Imaginary or "pretend games" were popular with a few; they also make and sell small objects or play bank, house and school. In more than a few instances, vestiges of these or related interests were sustained into adult life, and were translated into the network of factors influencing occupational choice. Guidance at the earlier ages might utilize such interests to advantage.

*Identifications*

The mechanism of identification generates power in both identity development and occupational choice. It is fascinating to watch the identification pendulum swing between the parents as it is governed by the stages.

The sixth graders or pre-adolescents who have heretofore been mother's "little girl" and the "delightful one" now have moments of moodiness and weeping. They "hang on" to mother or strike out at her verbally. In love with boys' games and tree climbing, they are also vain and spend long periods in front of the mirror.

[37]

Their fantasy material depicts mothers as either dead or distant while father figures take over her role; they rescue and protect their daughters. But fathers also steal, even from their wives. The stories seethe with ambivalence, but more positive feelings for father predominate.

When the former sixth graders were 14, and I talked with them again, their identifications were clearly and powerfully with peers. This seems to be part of their ardent efforts to sever old ties with parents. Identification with mother is quite negative; that with father more positive, but the girls complain that fathers are rarely at home. The erstwhile buoyant, vibrant sixth graders, now three years older, seem weighed down, apathetic and depressed. Bisexuality dominates sexual development, for this is the age of the crush.

Not only does the child identify with the parents; the latter identify the child with their own siblings, and sometimes encourage choice of occupations similar to those of the child's cousins. Mothers are still competing with sisters and using the child for this purpose. One girl reminded mother of her inlaws described in derogatory terms while another father's earliest memory of his daughter was her likeness to his mother — "a wonderful woman." So barren are some parents' identities that role models waver with the wind.

A third of the subjects introduced the topic of the individual's responsibility for what happens to her; a single and astute pre-adolescent, two mid-adolescents and two young adults spoke of this. Unfortunately I did not introduce it as a topic in the interview. Many take attitudes which suggest that occupation is something outside their orbit, a phenomenon that comes about through others. In pre-adolescence as well as throughout adolescence, many subjects react to the prospect of marriage as if they were worthless without such a state; their degree of confidence revolves around the occupation of the man. Our findings reinforce the view that the individual is both agent and reactor to

[38]

the positive and negative pressures of her life, as well as to her way of dealing with these pressures. More specifically, these reactions are discernible in the quality of coping mechanisms and defenses — an area where a good part of the change between the early and late testing took place. Compromise, perspective, and reality testing are positive, as of course is sublimation; while denial, rigidity, projection displacement and somatizing are more primitive.

The extended family, too, act as identification figures to the pre- and mid-adolescents. Some of the latter, along with four young adults, spoke ruefully of recently recognizing characteristics in themselves that they disliked in their mothers, finding that they, too, were often fussy about unimportant things, irritable and perfectionistic. What this means we are not certain. Possible interpretations are in Chapter 7.

Test protocols of the younger subjects are replete with oedipal struggles, adding weight to Blos' beliefs that girls, unlike boys, continue their romantic fantasies about their fathers throughout latency to mid-adolescence.

Erikson believes that identity is partly conscious, partly unconscious. It was primarily to glimpse components of the latter that I needed projective tests which tap a deeper level of personality. They also gave me a yardstick for measuring change in personality organization. Although there is a repository of rich data in the interview material, they can be supplemented appreciably by psychological test findings. Essentially these tests elicit fantasies or imaginative data; ways of perceiving and handling what they see in the Rorschach inkblots; and in the stories they tell about the more structured pictures in the TAT (Thematic Apperception Test). Machover Draw-A-Person focuses on self and body image; the Identity Sentence Completion in which the testee completes unfinished sentences; the Pigem Test which asks what the subject would like to be on returning to the world as *other* than a human being — all these reveal clues to the quality of thinking, inner dynamics, interpersonal relations and sense of self. Handwriting was analyzed in a few instances.

The case histories which follow were put together by the author from the recorded interviews with parents and teachers, from school reports, projective test data and, most important of all, from what the subjects themselves told me. Of the forty histories available I am presenting only six because of space limitations. Each girl or woman reported represents the stage or stages through which she is currently journeying. They are:

Lisa: a sixth grader
Pat: a high school senior
Mrs. V.: a young adult with a pioneer identity
Mrs. E.: another young adult but one who is atypical in the group
Miss S.: a mature and classic career woman
Mrs. N.: a retread nurse

In Chapter 3 which follows, Lisa represents the pre-adolescent girls whom I studied at two different intervals three years apart, starting when they were age eleven and in the sixth grade. My first impression of them centered on their zest, bounce, and excited enthusiasm. "Could they start a club out of it?" they asked.

This chapter deals with the individual girl as she talks about her activities, attitudes, feelings, ambitions, parents, and siblings. I hope to learn something of what she is like as an individual, and of some of the tributaries feeding into the stream of growing up. How accurately does she represent the group?

In contrast, Chapter 4 is focused on all ten girls who make up the group or unit of pre-adolescents, and the progress of these subjects in developing according to the Erikson stages of ego development. I call it Developmental Progress.

# PART II

## THE CASE HISTORIES

# CHAPTER 3
## Lisa: A Pre-adolescent at Age 11

The F's live in a charming, old restored house with a huge barn and small swimming pool — an ideal setting for a growing child. There is a brother, two years Lisa's senior; until last year, Lisa attended the same high-ranking suburban school. Now she and her brother are enrolled in excellent private schools. This is a family classified as upper middle-class; and one fairly free from stress of illness or money pressure.

*Background data*

Mrs. F (Lisa's mother) is a talkative, expansive lady somewhat dramatic, using extravagant language. She is self-assertive and humorous, and is rather repetitive. Quite frequently, Mrs. F compares herself with Lisa; she was however a more serious child than her daughter. Mrs. F's identification with Lisa is clear. Her father is a lawyer; and her sister is younger by six years. "My *mommy* brought us up in the good sense of the word like two only children, because we always had to consider the other child being around, but we really got a great deal of individual and very affectionate attention." Younger sister is unmarried and a social worker; their personalities are quite different. Mrs. F's parents thought she was a remarkable human being but they had very high standards, lots of lines to be toed, and certain arbitrarily chosen areas of behavior. "My mother likes children, is affectionate and attentive to my children also."

As a youngster, Mrs. F, like her daughter, was a "serious student" of both art and ballet. "But I think I shot my bolt by the time I was fourteen." She went to college as an art history

[43]

major. "But mostly I danced all over the place and had a marvelous time."

Then she met her husband in her junior year. "I quickly realized with considerable relief that you couldn't work and be married to a physicist." Before marriage she had gone to graduate school, majoring in art history. Then military service took them to a place where there were no job opportunities, so she renounced "artistic youth and settled down. I couldn't wait to have a child."

Some regrets about interrupting her career were suggested for practical reasons: "You've got to get enough of a start in whatever it is you're doing. I could be an art teacher now if I had been able to stay in graduate school." There has been a certain amount of freedom for Mrs. F through the hiring of sitters. "I certainly haven't spent the years sitting home — I'm much too restless for that. But as for having something that takes precedence in its demands on me, except for that year of work, I've never done it and have been glad not to have to."

In general, mother thinks careers for women can be quite compatible with marriage and children. "The specific field that Lisa is interested in, dance, is not an easy thing to go into, coming from our kind of family. When a child is slated for college and a certain kind of more socially acceptable career, even in an enlightened community, the dance is still declassé. I wanted to do this and I wouldn't stop Lisa, but there are a lot of worlds besides ours."

Of her husband, mother comments, "The most fantastic thing about my husband is that in spite of the fact that I have never really done anything since we were married, he regards me as somebody who is on her way to a career.

According to Mrs. F, her husband is rather quiet outside the home but really gentle, and "he still acts almost as if I were doing him a favor in doing his housework, which is really very nice." Dr. F is "very respectful of people's own potentials," she feels. "He lets our kids do what they want, he lets them express what they want; is very much in favor of encouraging every turn; never imposes the slightest notion of his own upon what they want." She dwells on his affection for Lisa in extravagant terms: "He was reduced to gibberish when he talked to her as a small child, sort of munching away at this delightful creature."

Superlatives abound in mother's perception of Lisa: she is a "remarkably determined human being, a very sound and very level-headed little girl, she's fantastic, even in this sort of a trying period she's very observant; knows what she wants and gets it usually in the most charming and painless way for everybody around. She has a great deal of energy, a great deal of self-reliance. She always has been able to sort of calm everybody down. One thing: she's extremely acquisitive; when she wants things, the world will end unless she gets them, but once she gets her own way, she's overflowing with understanding of everybody else."

As an infant, Lisa was "perfect, good natured and understanding; her brother is charming and temperamental." Lisa greatly resembles her grandmother in their shared openness, good nature, forcefulness and energy. So good-natured is Lisa that she tends to get imposed on by others. Because of her small size as a toddler she seemed precocious when talking at age two and has continued to be a verbal child.

At age three, she was being cared for by a teenage babysitter who was very unhappy. Lisa tried to cheer her up, thereby exchanging roles. This points up the recurring motif in Lisa's life of her concern, sensitivity and kindness to other people. "But she has a strong desire to conform; didn't like having her papers on the board because the kids called her 'teacher's pet'; she always wants everybody to love her, so is nice to them and avoids being different." This characteristic in Lisa reaches a point where mother feels she may be "squelching strong interests. She's been in a funny position because a lot of my ideas about how things

[45]

should be done or how little girls should be, run counter to what she sees around." Lisa's figure which is "round and plump" affects her present feelings about her appearance, and her prospects in ballet. "All she does is stand in front of the mirror and worry about what she looks like." This emphasis on weight and food is reflected in some of mother's phraseology, "such a delicious job, munching away at this delightful creature, a great big, fat thing." Her own mother is seriously overweight. Now Lisa's plumpness may hinder her going on from ballet to toe. "She'll end up a serious something, probably," said Mrs. F. "There's no stopping Lisa, she's absolutely self-propelled." Lisa's brother is similar to her in his whimsical, poetic imagination, but unlike Lisa, he is less thorough, productive and methodical. Mrs. F feels that perseverance, grit and determination are more important than talent.

A high level physicist, Dr. F is a trim-looking man of serious mien, but a somewhat morose quiet humor. Although he gives information conscientiously and thoughtfully, there seemed to be something rather isolated or uninvolved in his manner which is quite controlled. This may, however, be a shy reserve. There were two older sisters in father's family, as with mother's parents, the children are close to Dr. F's family; and his father is also a lawyer.

In comparing his present and childhood families, Dr. F thought that they are a little closer to their children. "My parents were rather wealthy and I was brought up by a nurse until I was eleven. I went to a private school which was across the big city from where I lived so that after school when I went home, I was by myself. And I didn't have quite the same contact with my parents that I think our kids have with us. But it is not terribly or drastically different."

From the time of his early high school days, Dr. F knew that he would pursue a career in research physics. "I think my own life is pretty ideal for me right now; it's a very selfish life, I must admit, to realize some of my own creative feelings and to be able to do my work, scientific work which is more or less creative." He recalls Lisa as a baby on vacations as "very active, never whined, never a spoiled child. Her mood was always good, never morose or withdrawn, always outgoing; she liked people, talked to everybody." As a younger child Lisa played both alone and with others. She always had her brother as a playmate and preferred imaginative to structured games. "She loves to read. At times, she expresses loud resistance to carrying out requests, but acquiesces in the end." She has "a certain facility for learning the piano, is no great genius at it." There is a challenge in trying "to do better than the next guy, and to please the teacher, and she dances very well, has been taking lessons since age six and a half; is an excellent swimmer."

Lisa has aways liked school and has done well. Whether self-motivated or to please her father he was uncertain, but "she's been doing extra work in science. How much of it she understands, I don't know. She is always quick to point out various scientific things that she sees in nature which is sort of nice. But she was never a great collector of any kind.

"We don't do the kids' homework for them but we show them how they can do it for themselves. Lisa will probably finish college and may have a career." In general he thinks she's too young to know. While she takes a variety of lessons, she has never expressed a wish to continue with these things as a career or in any serious way as a hobby. "I think she enjoys the dancing; wants to do well in it, just for the sake of doing well."

When she gets to college Lisa will probably decide what her career interests are. Dr. F's preference is expressed straightforwardly: "I've always had a preference for things scientific because that's what I understand best and I'd like to sort of project myself. If she went into something scientific, it would please me a great deal, but anything in which she can realize her own potentialities would also be gratifying." Activity with boys is limited to skating and to boy-girl parties. Thus far, father has not felt the issue to be a problem.

There is mutual admiration by her brother on the basis of Lisa's cleverness and niceness and Lisa for his athletic prowess. "But from an early age he resented her. She was rather pretty and admired and threatened his little kingdom, so he's always taken a pop at her every now and then, he teases her. Now that they are growing up, they like each other's company." Lisa's brother has never been as successful in school as she. "He's always had a lot of competition, whereas she's sort of had it easy."

Lisa is a charming looking, rather short, plump girl with cherubic features, an olive skin and a zestful, friendly manner. Usually she is alight with glow, but at other times, there is an impression of languidness. She articulates well and has a delightful sense of humor about herself. Asked to describe herself, she gave the opinion of a friend who said, "I am short and I like to laugh a lot, and have a pretty good sense of humor. Sometimes I get carried away with myself and try to be the best person, but I try to be fair and try to make people like me by being nice to them." Lisa tells of her wish next summer at camp to help a newcomer to "adjust" should she notice one who looks frightened as she was the first year. Her most admired classmate is a girl who is "nice to everybody and gets along well with everybody. She's smart but doesn't show off at all and she's very pretty and tall. She just got back from Europe and really had a good time. I had a lot of fun talking to her about it." Travel is of particular interest to Lisa, who has been fascinated with the slides of her parents' trips and people in foreign lands. "I would like to sort of be an ambassador, for myself."

A spate of interests and activities crowd Lisa's life. She rides, swims, collects post cards and china knick-knacks. As a younger child she used to play with some favorite dolls, look at picture books and watch television. "My mother says I had my fill of TV when I was little and it's not good for us." Favorite pastimes were watching brother play baseball, running along the beach and seeing the shells.

"I don't really enjoy keeping house but I don't get ferocious about it. I'd try to avoid anything when it comes to housekeeping, but I'll probably adjust too."

When she had to decide whether to ride a pony as she usually did or get on a horse, "I got on the horse and I was almost petrified but I was very excited." This is but one illustration of Lisa's desire to learn and grow and also of her free and honest expression of her feelings. There is, however, also a tendency to say what she thinks is expected.

Social studies and science are special favorites. "It's really interesting to read books about Newton and Pasteur and other people who tried to express their ideas when the odds were against them." And she likes writing descriptive themes.

Lisa wants to go to private school for a couple of years because it's more fun and something different. "You can really say more things in class and can express your ideas about nature and everything. And I think the curriculms (sic) are better."

When she is 19 or 20, Lisa thinks she may want to be a law secretary, but does not commit herself to this for more than a year or so to "add income" until she marries. Ideas about being a legal secretary probably derive partly from her admired grandfather who is a judge and from watching the TV program, *Perry Mason*. Another admired person is grandmother because she "gets around, really tries to help people and she is always making things to send overseas and other work."

Lisa thinks she might get married and if she does would like to work for the first couple of years for the income. Maybe two children would be a good number but definitely an even number so that no child could feel in the middle or left out and they could be good companions. Asked about decision making, Lisa commented, "I think that as somebody grows older, they should make their own decisions for themselves and not always lean on

[49]

one person because sometimes you won't always be with that same person."

*Lisa from the viewpoint of the school*

At the outset in kindergarten, her teacher describes her as very likable, extraverted personality with varied interests — "can make a game of anything and is willing to try new things; is self-confident and not thwarted by failure and takes criticism calmly and with apologies."

The general tenor of these comments reappear in the next grades: "Very regular child appealing to children and adults alike; takes things in her stride, rarely cries — takes work quite seriously and has made rapid progress, a good organizer and leader; highly imaginative and creative with good sense of rhythm, always follows through; strong desire to learn; has a wonderful quality of sympathy and understanding."

The only upsetting incident took place when mother did not have her dress ready for a recital Lisa was giving. She is sensitive to classmates, popular with boys, though career-minded.

*Impressions of identity formation from projective tests*

Ambitious, extremely bright, and well-controlled, Lisa unfolds a rich vein of fantasy which she enjoys using and which serves her well in the predigesting of experiences and in mulling things over. Balancing this, is down-to-earth, conventional thinking which is well structured.

Lisa is extremely responsive emotionally, intensely alive and open to all sorts of stimuli. Most outstanding is her hypersensitivity, and in this she seems mature beyond her years, even over-socialized, with an especially strong need for affection and response. The impact of the environment makes her vulnerable, anxious, even contributes a feeling of rawness in being exposed. Yet this need for response is controlled; and also contributes a rather unusual (in this stage and age group) ability to empathize.

[50]

But when she is told by her singing coach that she is offkey (on a TAT story) she never learns to sing no matter how she tries.

Lisa identifies with the wise owls she sees on the Rorschach. The fiercer animals are described as "little" while the harmless butterflies are called "big." This may serve to diminish the threat of instinctual life; she is also concerned with size (her own?) There is a tendency to envisage others as big and significant in relation to her "smallness."

There are suggestions of beginning adolescent friction with mother, as in spending money for clothes unwisely in order to be like the other girls, since mother had formerly made all of Lisa's clothes. But there is also considerable positive identification with mother, as well as with father and brother. In one story, she and brother have no money, for their parents have died. They consult a soothsayer who reassures them. But they decide never to marry. Is brother replacing father in the oedipal involvement?

An especially prominent theme deals with money, possessions, and gifts. Invariably parents are described as either rich or poor; at times the latter inherit money. Does this signify a strong receptive tendency and feelings of deprivation, or exorbitant need for outer support (dependency), and power through an acquisitive drive? Does money symbolize love to Lisa who is so hungry for response?

Poverty usually results from the death of the parents. In one story, however, a rich little girl renounces luxury to study and become a dancer. Frequent stories point up an inner unrest and turmoil; there are suggestions of fears of the dark, but Lisa meets this by investigating the supposed danger, taking action rather than passively accepting her fears. Friends, too, help to assuage the anxiety. Unlike most others her age, she says on the Sentence Completion Test that she does not like boys.

The ideal person she draws is a camp counselor — "smart, thin, and pretty." Wishes of the self representation are realistic and conventional, "to be popular, a leader, pretty, have boy

[51]

friends, and no skin problems, and do well in school." Eyes receive special emphasis pointing up the watchfulness and observant qualities, as well as being watched by others.

What she would *most* like to be if she couldn't be human: "a horse because I would like to know how they feel when they get the crop and be nice to my rider"; *least,* a skunk "because everybody hates them and I would smell bad."

Lisa's feelings about men and boys are quite mixed; they are both dangerous and protective; she is drawn toward them yet fears sexuality. There is, however, fair acceptance of her sex role and of herself in general. What stands out in the protocol is the good degree of balance among her various characteristics. This balance and taste are graphically illustrated in her handwriting.

Progress toward identity seems to move with more forward than backward steps, athough the latter are clearly present. Like many girls her age, she overvalues what others think, her hypersensitivity to feelings of others confuses the boundary of her ego, and suggests the large-sized need for affection.

*Transactions among family members and Lisa's identification pattern*

Dr. F is a reserved man, studious, quite, low key and self-contained. His wife in contrast is quite outspoken, dynamic, confident, hyperbolic and gregarious. Despite the contrast in temperaments, the parents appear to communicate well, both with each other and with the children. The marriage seems to be a congenial one with mutual respect and a great deal of warmth toward and involvement with the children. Father's expressed appreciation of Mrs. F's role as housewife, as well as his admiration for her talents are most unusual. He makes her feel important as a woman. The children here probably absorbed security and a favorable conception of marriage from the relationship between the parents. There is a sharing of many acti-

[52]

vities, interests and ideas among the family members but also a good degree of freedom for each one to develop his own potentialities and interests. Parents perceive Lisa quite similarly, with father more down to earth and realistic about her abilities. Lisa has repeated Mrs. F's experience in ballet and the latter understandably has strong feelings about it. The more dominant parent is Mrs. F — although her husband certainly influences the family in a subtle way. Lisa is treated by both parents mostly as an individual. They tend to foster although not insist on characteristics in line with their own particular talents and interests.

Although closely identified with her mother, there is also some degree of identification with Dr. F and brother. These identifications seem to be predominantly positive and fairly comfortable. Resemblances to mother are seen in Lisa's talkativeness, exuberance and concern for the effect of her words on others. Like mother, Lisa is ambitious, but rarely expresses it directly because it clashes with the current mores of her friends. At this time, affiliation drive seems uppermost. Likenesses to father are Lisa's studious, creative and independent qualities as well as control. Mother appears quite comfortable in her femininity and has fostered this in Lisa. Lisa says on one test, "The best thing about being a girl is wearing pretty clothes and becoming a woman." Men are pictured as both dangerous and protective, but not violent.

Peer and group identifications *have* been emphasized, and take the form of a wish for a nice figure and close friends. She has one or two close, rather than many friends. She does her homework under the living room table because she "likes to be near us" according to Mrs. F. Closeness is especially important to Lisa; as is a desire to help others, which seems more usual at adolescence.

[53]

*Ego development and journey through the stages*

A delightful, even-tempered child from the beginning, Lisa has developed a sound sense of trust. She is optimistic and self-confident and has a remarkable degree of empathy for her fellow human beings. There is a good balance between giving and taking in her relations with others. If the gifts and inheritances so frequently mentioned in the TAT suggest a receptive trend, the ratio favoring trust would be reduced. Yet it definitely tends toward the positive side; she was a wanted child.

As a toddler, Lisa continued to seek out and trust others. She is determined, though not stubborn, has good control but is flexible, spontaneous, yet at times irritable. One actual parental value is simplicity; making do with a single bathroom and retaining a car year after year without trading it. Lisa disagrees with these values, preferring luxuries. In decision-making, she is not afraid to depend on others for advice but is thoughtful and likes to make independent decisions. Autonomy predominates over shame and guilt. Her will and control appear to have flourished.

In the initiative stage, Lisa developed the roots of a positive and rather close sex identification. Most of the rivalry emanated from brother. There are indications of ambivalent feelings toward men which is not unusual at this level. Her talents and exploratory activities are not restricted by guilt. Lisa is now quite absorbed in her physical appearance and in making herself attractive. In her love of dramatics in school, her piano recitals, and ballet, there may be an element of exhibitionism to which she applies the brake of reaction formation by her dislike for "showing off" and her conformity. Initiative predominates over guilt.

She is doing well in the industry period with rapid progress in school work and satisfaction in the challenge of meeting standards. At the other polarity, there are feelings of uncertainty, even inferiority but these seem to be fairly transient.

[54]

Now in pre-adolescence, she is displaying phase-specific characteristics in her turn to and adaptation toward reality, her play-acting, interest in clothes, and her activity. Although she joins her peers in talking about boys, and moves toward heterosexuality by dating a little, her feelings are mixed. All of the above provide weapons for use against the phase-specific regressive pull back to the caretaking (physical) mother of the earlier years to whom girls in this stage retreat as the activity of boy-girl relationships move closer and are frightening. That mother is sensitive to her needs and available to her, helps Lisa to resist the pull.

In general, there is strong evidence of a "growing together" and relative mastery of experiences, with the development of well defined direction and purpose in life and marked self-awareness and self acceptance for a girl her age. Personal identity has evolved at a fast pace. But although identifications with mother, father and grandparents are clear, Lisa is not a "carbon-copy" of any one and very much an individual in her own right. Drives are quite insistent and imperious, but her control seems adequate. Her own convictions will probably superordinate the tendency to be what others want her to be.

Lisa has a sound foundation of identity on which to build. Her orientation will likely be double or triple track. An interesting common theme is found in the fact that both parents and grandparents regard their children as something special.

*Lisa three years later*

To set up the interview with Lisa, I telephoned her home and spoke with Mrs. F who told me of her own return to graduate school. The best way to describe Lisa, she said, is "cool" — not a worrier like her mother and brother. Lisa sees herself as opposite. She loves to explore the city and spends time at Harvard Square, enjoys eating and being with friends but rarely dates except for school parties. Mother feels that she weighs too much, and that this influenced her decision to discontinue her ballet lessons. Lisa implemented this without discussing it at home,

[55]

announcing it quite calmly. It wasn't worth the sacrifice, she said, especially since she felt that her talent, while substantial, was not up to that of a first-class ballerina. The sacrifice entailed constant dieting as well as expenditure of time. Mother said that menarche had not yet taken place. At 14, Lisa's appearance has changed; she is still somewhat short and plump with well-formed features and bright eyes, but the glow of the earlier years is no longer so striking. As before, she leans on her elbow and yawns a lot. Nor is she as responsive, although she is conscientious and eases up as the interview progresses.

"The most important happening of the last three years is the change of school. I think C. [private school] is great. I like it better than I would have liked any other school. It is small and you get to know everybody and the kids have parties for the whole school. There's a greater concentration of interest in the studies — the teachers try to make it interesting, and the kids go there because they want to work. This isn't true of a public school."

Her best areas are in English, French, and Biology; poorest is Math. "And I really like the Headmaster. He's more intelligent than most adults, and is devoting his life to working with kids who are smart but couldn't get a good education, like a classmate from Mississippi. And he isn't rigid, gives the kids both leeway and responsibility. In the sixth grade, I had only one very good friend, but in the seventh she was in a different division, so I rarely saw her, and then she moved away. Then I didn't have a single close friend in junior high. Now all my friends are at my new school, and they live mostly in different towns.

"I'm very interested in writing and linguistics, sort of etymological stuff." English has always been a favorite; she might go into journalism. "This summer we went to Europe so I liked speaking languages." The outstanding event of the trip was

[56]

meeting the singing group, the Rolling Stones, and other nice people.

"I'm also interested in ceramics, spend most of my time after school at it now that I've stopped my dancing which took up six days a week." Yes, she does sort of regret it, but now she can study more and work at potting. "You have to be very, very good to join any sort of ballet company and spend all of your time at it." It is interesting that mother's dance performance also worsened at age fourteen. "I guess academic work is good enough for me. I love the city and seeing all sorts of people, and walking around; it's much more beautiful than the suburbs."

Lisa bypassed most of the interviewer's questions as to what she was like and how she had changed. She was sort of adventurous, and felt older than most kids in her class. "It's sort of philosophical thinking, sitting around and drawing." What did she think about? "About everything, — mostly about courses in school because you have to decide how much you are going to put into each. All kids are striving for an adult point of view." No, her parents could not help her with her school work. "They have almost *nothing* to do with my school affairs. This is good as long as I am reasonable in planning. I think anyone in the ninth grade at my school is capable of timing their affairs and having reasonable social and academic balance. I try to be humorous, can't stand it the way some people are dead-pan; you need a good balance of pensiveness and humor." Even though it's easy to make friends at C., the kids really discuss their problems and are not "socially inhibited." There are no cliques and Lisa feels it best not to affiliate oneself too greatly with anything. "When maturity comes, there is a lot less adolescent criticizing of friends, *biting* into them. If you take a reasonable approach to your problems, you don't get all tensed up and scream at your friends and your mother. In the sixth grade, at the other school, there were a lot of firm, clannish, brutal cliques, really catty. It was sort of stupid." In Lisa's version, she displaces the focus of

[57]

her school work from her mother to her "pompous" teachers at junior high.

Her mother doesn't get home from college until dinner time, her brother too. She herself is busy until late afternoon, and her father is rarely home because he is busy on some new research. "I don't spend much time just sitting and gabbing with my mother and speaking about problems; we never have time. But I'm glad she's studying. A lot of adolescents feel apathy for adults because of the power image. If you are exposed to people who are reasonable and wonderful, it all falls into place. But there are some stupid, pompous teachers in the school system. My brother and I have differences, but basically we're friends.

"Actually I'm not as reasonable as I make myself out; some of it is wishful thinking. I'm sort of a heel a lot of the time at home and get irritable. There's a strain on everybody — we're all working hard. I don't kill myself studying, but I'm serious about college, a fairly prestigious one. If you're going to have a family, you should really work in graduate school, and once you finish taking care of your family, say when they are fifteen, go back to work." Lisa guesses she'd have four or five children, not three because the middle child is always unhappy.

Rather than medicine, Lisa is drawn to psychoanalysis. "I love to criticize people eloquently like Mary McCarthy [the author], and had thought seriously of becoming a dance critic because I write well, besides knowing a lot about dancing."

About her newly born niece, Lisa says, "I really didn't like kids but this one is all right. They look so much like animals when they are little. I prefer the ones from two to four — old enough to play with." She would like to rear her children as she was brought up, but is not sure she's capable because she's more nervous than Mrs. F. "My mother let us go out on our own and develop independently. Besides, I want to get a firm grasp on what I'm going to do with my life before I go back to staying at home."

[58]

Many changes in Lisa over the three-year period stand out: the heightened self-awareness, the growth in her thoughtfulness about future career, and her well-integrated, innovative ideas about what it will be, plus her new independence especially from what people think of her, and her honesty.

The Headmaster of Lisa's new school describes her as one of the most respected students despite a quick temper and a sharp tongue. She has a high quality of intelligence and a solid judgment. At times she deflates the unrealistic ideas of other students, yet has many friends of both sexes. Her emphasis on friends seems a bit excessive, he thinks. She is an independent thinker — a spark rather than a follower — and always in the thick of things. She ranks scholastically toward the upper half of a very competitive group.

Lisa is pulled in opposite directions, a tug-of-war between un-involvement on the one hand and considerable empathy on the other. Marriage is now viewed as delayed until after some success at work. Formerly, work was temporary and its purpose was to earn money.

Tentatively, it would seem that a journalistic career centering around the use of words may provide some sublimation for the clear-cut oral components in her history. Here a model has been provided by mother and maternal grandmother. At school, her intellectual side has been mobilized and she has additional identification figures of apparently high values. Her strongest identifications are, however, chiefly with her peers, and this is age-specific.

*Interpenetration of identity formation and occupational role; aspects of psychological and work dynamics*

From the very early days, Lisa caught from her parents a sense of her own worth. As father said, Lisa's urge to achieve derived from pride of workmanship itself. Yet while her aspiration level has risen, her degree of commitment now varies and fluctuates. This is not evident in her earlier thoughts about occupations; but were more stereotyped and based on copying real teenagers whom she admired, also perhaps on her tight grasp onto her image — a self-loving one in early adolescence.

Now — three years later — Lisa wants to be a dance critic or journalist. But she doesn't want to be a "brain" or "teacher's pet." Thus she restricts her ego functioning, and doesn't go all-out in her activities, for this would down-grade her with peers.

The extraordinary part of her new, though tentative goal rests on the insight with which she puts pieces of herself together to arrive at a perspicacious, imaginative and innovative synthesis — *the goal of the dance critic.* It is probably based, too, on identification with the journalist Mary McCarthy. But she also adds a practical touch: her enjoyment of and flair for writing.

Lisa values the reasonable, thinking, reading individual, emphasizes the ego. Then in her honesty she acknowledges the other side of the coin — speaking of her irritability, especially toward her mother. She has an occupational image of herself in a top-level job both before and after marriage, a pattern rare in this group. Apparently Lisa has strong angry feelings which she tries to control and to sublimate. Becoming a critic furnishes a socially acceptable role for this, and she tries to oppose her rage by repeating it and to curb her ambition by lowering her goals.

Even the advent of a child would take up too much of her life. It is as if she might lose something of her physical self by investing in phases of life. Again this may reflect the phase-specific and heightened narcissistic drive of early adolescence when pressures of impulse expression rise. Her parents appear to be "good" role models in their encouragement of work and school as values, and have allowed the freedom Lisa needs in growing up occupationally. At fourteen, when characteristics of the stage of early adolescence would be expected, Lisa demonstrates those of the more advanced identity stage as well as glimpses of late adolescence. The beginnings of integration of identifications, and consolidation are visible. Ego growth is clearly advanced, and she aspires to a sophisticated profession.

Her anger at being left out by the hated cliques at her first school still riles; it seems related to being left by her only girl friend moving away — a bereft feeling. When a theme is repeated in the second series of tests, as in Lisa's protocols emphasizing money, it probably has real meaning which was suggested in reporting the first test results. Success follows attendance at the best school. Identification, positive and negative, with mother is strongly suggested from her stated desires to rear her own family in the way she was raised. Formerly somewhat interested in Dr. F's field, she now calls science "stupid" and comments on his frequent absence from home. There is reluctance to talk about whom she is like, but the strongest current identification is with her peers.

A journalistic career centering around the use of words may provide some sublimation for the clear-cut oral components manifested by her love of food and use of such words as "biting." This is even more prominent in Mrs. F's use of language.

*Blind comparison of 1964 and 1967 projective test protocols*

In the three years since 1964, Lisa's sense of identity, both generally and in terms of occupational goals, has changed and matured strikingly. Over this period of time and through the zig-zag course of the early adolescent years, certain constants in Lisa's personality stand out. She is basically a bright, sensitive and charming girl, responsive to the emotional nuances of her world. In '64 and '67 she appears both quite aware of the competitive potential of life and somewhat unsure of herself and her abilities. But the manner in which she handles her insecurities, both on the level of fantasy and actual behavior, has changed quite dramatically, as have her avowed attitudes toward life and her goals for her future.

In '64, Lisa had a rather clearly defined picture of herself as

[61]

a composed but relatively inept person. She wanted to do well but felt somewhat overwhelmed and unsure. She appeared responsive to her own feelings and aware of her deep wish to be popular and successful. Whenever she felt the need for support in '64, she sought it in the form of parental and peer approval, was then willing and able to use her initiative and strike out.

Her goals at that time were rather traditional, she wanted to be a success in studies, sports and socially. The competition that mainly preoccupied her in '64 was that over boys. This aim extended to her ideas concerning her adult future. She aimed at becoming a loved wife and a happy mother. In '67, Lisa and her ideal are much more alike, even wear identical clothes. Both are subdued, subtle personalities, cerebral, aloof and idealistic. Now she is more comfortable in being herself. The '67 ideal goes to college and graduate school, then becomes an artist or a literary person. (This is clearly Lisa's current plan for living.) Now she would most like to be a swan rather than the horse of '64. "It is pretty and independent, but also aloof."

In '67 Lisa's dependence is much less on her parents than on her own ability, although there are subtle suggestions that she is not as independent as she would like to be. She has quite clear ideas now that while she does want comfort and affluence, she is mainly interested in acquiring a new sense of success. She is less interested in competing for boys now or for aiming at a life of happy domesticity. Now she wants the gratifications of intellectual achievement. She sees her fulfillment not in babies and a home, but in a "literary" career after graduate work in theology or philosophy. The thinking life is her highest personal value.

As Lisa unfolds for us these changes in her attitude about life, love and personal success several things become clear. In '64, when she began grappling with the pre-adolescent struggle over heterosexuality and facing the emotional impact of sex, Lisa was frightened. More especially she feared the sexually aggressive aspect of masculinity and how it might hurt or molest her. This

[62]

fear was greater in the '64 protocols, partly because of Lisa's free access to her feelings. But it also reflected her own strong ambivalence over her feelings toward men.

As Lisa comes into early adolescence, her ways of dealing with these fears appear quite different. There is less aggressive masculinity in her "other sex" drawings. Now Lisa denies and converts her fears — she has developed reaction-formation against them and has shifted and displaced her emotional involvement "upward." Her main preoccupation now is not boys but ideas.

She no longer shows the extreme tact and need to please, is now more egocentric and preoccupied with the impulse expression so characteristic of the early adolescent. Phase-specific, too, is the stress on the satisfaction of having friends now — a problem area for her in '64. And dating in a group supports her.

There is massive counteraction; her hostility is more modulated and differentiated and so is her identity. The togetherness has modified and she emphasizes her independence from parents which is phase-specific; the parents seem to take this in stride since their own identities are solidly formed. Her friends at school and her teachers offer substitute ego ideals which support her. The need to conform has diminished. It may be that some aspect of nurturance will be part of her occupational identity. Whatever Lisa does, she will be an active participant in the fashioning of her life.

Some of what the '64 protocols show indicate that the demands of such an identity struggle shake Lisa emotionally. Often times she yearns for a closeness for which she has not yet grown capable. She often doubts herself and is now (in contrast to '64) much more introspective than reactive, more reflective and at times lonely. Controls are well developed. She handles aggression by toning it down and reversing it to a helping rather than a hurting situation, or using coping mechanisms of identification and sublimation and only occasionally explodes.

SYLVIA KORSTVEDT, PH.D.
*Clinical Psychologist*

[63]

# CHAPTER 4
## The Developmental Progress
## of the Group of Pre-adolescents

In the detailed life histories, I have highlighted the quality of uniqueness, the ideographic way in which outer circumstances and inner forces penetrate each other. This investigation, on the other hand, deals with group trends in identity growth at two Erikson stages: pre-adolescent (age 11) and early adolescence (14). It reports the regularities within the groups and what in general their concerns seem to be. Similar presentations of each of the groups will follow along with illustrations of that growth.

There was space enough to give histories in full for only one case in each stage except for the shorter ones of the young adults. The trends to be discussed are, however, derived and calculated on the basis of ten histories in each group, or forty in all.

The subjects' families fall mostly in the upper-middle social class and are notably upward-striving. Except for a few, they own their single family homes, a number of which are new, pleasant, and spacious. Subjects have attended schools in a suburban section with a high rating. With this group the strains of World War II were experienced by half of the fathers. One father was wounded, and many had been away from home for considerable periods.

Formal education of the mothers ranges from one who is a physician, two with a graduate school background, and a few who had not completed high school. But they expect their daughters to go to college and to achieve. One mother recites poetry to her child while driving her to school, to impart culture. With the exception of two girls, all are doing well.

All but one of the mothers worked before marriage; she was

[64]

in graduate school. Their occupations spanned a wide territory: combination dancer and accompanist for a band, a cluster of sales and semi-skilled workers. A teacher and a psychiatrist have continued to work part-time.

Most of the fathers have achieved an above average degree of financial success in professions or management rank; one is a high-level physicist. Night work is frequent and the girls see their fathers rarely. This predominates to an even greater extent in the Group II girls, the mid-adolescents. One father said rather enigmatically, "Even when I am home I am hard to find."

While about half of the mothers seem attuned to their daughters' concerns, a third of them gave priority to their own ambitions in talking of possible choices. Though critical of boy-girl parties, they react strongly when their daughter is not invited, or deviates from the group in some way. Social skills are valued; the girls take all sorts of "lessons" in addition to their school work. A few of the mothers feel that their child is particularly unsophisticated while at the same time these very girls are talking about their experiences in the "make-out" clubs in school. Times of acute friction with their daughters have not yet arrived although these are anticipated. "Last year she was easier, less demanding. Now she sits in front of the mirror for hours, and tends to cry a lot." Yet the mothers generally describe their daughters with affection: "a little family girl; simply delightful; a delicious pixie." Only two used such terms as "demanding and bossy like my mother-in-law."

More than half of the fathers verbalized sparsely about possible careers for their daughters. "I guess I still think of her as my little girl." Yet in other ways a few encourage sophisticated activities. One took his daughter to a New York night club where she danced the twist with a stranger. Others had a limited perception of careers, regarding work as insurance of a job should the need arise; or as useful in helping husband in his business. Such a

[65]

conception of work is not very stirring to 11-year-old girls. But while the girls evaded discussions of jobs, they participate more in the concrete. In more than a third of the cases, communication between parents seems somewhat strained and the husband takes rather arbitrary stands. One insisted that his wife drop out of a part-time continuing education program.

Three of the girls are excellent athletes; one loves to play-act, another to play school, a third enjoys the game of doctor. Two gifted girls could "sing and dance" all day; one of these loves to cook and to draw. "I'm a great reader," said another. The girls enjoy working together on school projects. Eleven seems to be an age of heightened alertness to everything that goes on at home; they are "all ears." Most fourteen-year-olds make a clear distinction between career and marriage; but the pre-adolescents do not visualize the double track. "If I don't get married, I may be a scientist." Practically all of the girls placed marriage at the center of their lives.

Almost two-thirds of the subjects do well in school, are considered bright by their teachers, and more than half are described as cooperative, hard working, and conscientious, but somewhat underachieving. Special aptitudes are recognized early; and a fifth of the sample were described as "genuinely disturbed" by teachers. Although mothers had emphasized their daughters' love for school, some of the girls had different ideas, one writing in huge letters on the blackboard: "I hate school." Some were quite unhappy over their dearth of close friends who serve as confidants and set the model for behavior in social situations. One in this group transferred to a private school because she felt outside of the group.

*Impressions from projective tests*

The seeds of intense rivalry with mothers come through quite clearly in the tests, far more than in interviews. For these girls are close to and still dependent on mothers, a combination which

[66]

makes it difficult to express hostility directly. The cardinal feeling is one of beginning ambivalence. They present their feelings on the tests by eliminating mothers from stories through death or divorce or disappearance or by making her a mean stepmother, or an adoptive mother, or by putting fathers in her role. The latter get star billing for rescuing daughters. Typically, the oedipal involvement is prominent. Although father figures are seen as kings, these images of men have a second side; they cheat, steal daughters' jewels, assault and sometimes kill; are perhaps a source of considerable anxiety over loss of body intactness. At this age, identification with fathers seems far stronger and more positive. He is the giving parent, showering his daughter with gifts. Form perception is more accurate suggesting a better sense of reality at 14.

Another new and prominent theme at 14 deals with that of adoption. This seems to overlay fantasies of being of royal blood, a queen or princess; and fancies that a girl's current parents are not her real ones.

Popularity is one of the strongest, most frequent strivings of this group. It is often achieved through finding a popular boy friend, or in fewer instances through the girl's own efforts and virtuosity or her beauty.

Sharing confidences about boys with their girl friends seems to be more fun than having dates themselves. From the phase-specific viewpoint the girls have mixed sex identifications. The subjects at eleven seem to be saying: "My parents do not understand or appreciate me, for they are not really my parents — I am adopted. Yet I need them, for life is somewhat scary, especially when dating starts. What I want is to get married and have children. And I'll do a better job bringing them up than my mother did."

Impulses at this age clamor imperiously but are not expressed on a conscious level. There is also an achievement motivation, and certain values internalized from parents — some positive,

[67]

others negative. If the former holds, some control over impulses results.

Career is a poor second choice which means that it is virtually equated with failure in dating. Almost all have trouble visualizing the double track; or respond as if they have never heard of it.

*Journey through the stages*

Erikson conceives the end of the latency period as marking the ascendency of a sense of industry characterized by satisfaction in completing tasks, by wanting to be useful, and working in a team with others. At this time the child learns to win recognition by producing things and developing skills. If she fails, the danger lies in a sense of inferiority. School is the chief arena for the development of industry. The bulk of the girls appear to be making progress in this area. With a few, the danger of inferiority predominates.

Slightly more than half met the tasks of each stage generally on schedule, even though relics of incompletely resolved earlier stages persist. Dissolution of these conflicts may be mastered in later stages. Half of the girls seem to be consistently slow in meeting crises.

Blos (1962) presents pre-adolescence as a phase when a decisive turn to reality and an intensive process of adaptation takes place. Playacting and tomboy activities testify to a girl's renunciation of infantile fantasy. The anxiety and inhibition she encounters when she turns to reality (prospect of dating and so forth) brings her back to the care-taking mother for a period "marked by heightened and more infantile demands which make liberation more difficult." The girl at this stage defends herself by a decisive turn to heterosexuality. Yet she cannot be called feminine since she is so often the aggressor and seducer in the pseudo game of love. Should the girl surrender, and act out the regression by displacement or succumb to the regressive pull, a

[68]

deviate adolescence follows. The aegis under which positive development occurs is the liberation from the mother which enables the girl to resist the regression.

The locale for this reaching out seems to be largely in the social sphere. Acceptance by peers assumes high importance. It seems that these girls cannot feel *real* unless accepted by others, both girls and boys, and that this acceptance in turn hinges on freeing themselves from parents, especially from mothers; and moving forward to an arena larger than the home.

*The girls three years later*

When the subjects returned for retesting and a follow-up talk at age fourteen, they were in the early adolescent stage. A few had changed in appearance and manner so markedly that they seemed like different girls. The former bouncy quality and sense of excitement had been replaced by apathy and flatness; they presented a dismal picture of their current lives. "Nothing at all has happened" or "we don't have much fun" or "life is dull and boring" — seemed to be the characteristic reaction. The boys at junior high were too short, they complained, and "not very interesting."

Age 14 brings some advance in their capacity to define future occupational roles more realistically, and to do so in the context of a growing knowledge of themselves. One with a former teaching goal had decided that she did not want to go to school for the length of time required; she hated school. Moreover she hoped to marry at nineteen and wanted an "easy" job. Another had wisely decided that she was not ready to make a decision. But beyond all is the reiteration of their primary desire to marry; a few feared almost superstitiously that even a tentative consideration of future occupational role might interfere with their major one.

The flat and apathetic aspects corresponded to reactions to projective tests; now at fourteen their responses have an impoverished quality. Two girls have displaced anxiety in an upward direction; they use intellectualization and are now doing excellent work in school. Predominant mood is one of sadness, frustration, and depression. The dark mood seems closely related to loss — fancies of loss of parents in an accident, or loss of children.

Pre-adolescents and early adolescents give a paucity of information, not only in expressing goals other than marriage, but in giving reasons for their choices. "I just like it" or "I don't know why," they say. The phase-specific longing of girls at these stages for popularity also appears mostly in the protocols, as did the parental forcing theme. Projective tests were sorely needed and helpful in suggesting what the subject does not know so cannot say; also what she does know but cannot or *will not* express. Clearer, too, are the themes which preoccupy her, as well as her way of handling difficulties.

When we met with the early adolescents now 14 years old in a *group*, however, the interaction became lively and spontaneous. Individual members were able to express antagonism for parents and relate it to "pestering about homework," and to many rules about dating or other restrictions. Into the open, too, came their bisexual interest in both boys and girls, and their intense curiosity about illicit sexuality.

With a few exceptions, occupations were considered transient way stations on the road to marriage or as related to the husband's ability to support them — an echo of the fathers' attitudes. The exceptions were chiefly the especially bright girls and superior students who truly wanted to use their minds. It would seem that the phase-specific process of loosening attachments is equated with a general sense of loss which involves grief and real suffering.

Even stronger ties to girl friends help take up the slack in parental relationships at 14, assuming the form of crushes or "ideal persons." Two girls had exchanged necklaces to symbolize

[70]

that they were "going steady." Secrets too are a prevalent form of communication. Stories dealing with romance have increased, but often end unhappily. Bisexuality still plagues, and fixity of sex role awaits greater resolution of oedipal dilemmas. Antagonism toward mothers, however, is expressed in more muted tones than later.

Again these findings correspond quite accurately with Blos' (1962) presentation of early adolescence, with its weaker super-ego by virtue of a diminished tendency to internalize parental values, its depressed mood and combination of void and turmoil. Attachments (to girl friends) are modeled on the self — a form of narcissism, and the subjects ponder over whether they are boys or girls. "Friendships, crushes, fantasy life, intellectual interests, athletic activities, interest in grooming — all protect the girl from precocious dating, that is, a defensive heterosexuality." The emotional availability of the parent, particularly the mother is, however, the girl's ultimate safeguard.

So uncommunicative were the girls at fourteen in interviews that we were fortunate in having the projective data. Meeting with the subjects in a group was also productive. Two girls said nothing throughout the two-hour session; the others appeared stimulated and talked far more freely than in the individual interviews.

Some form of group guidance oriented around such topics as self-awareness, or what my life will be like in fifteen years, rather than around occupational choice, might be more effective than individual counseling at this age. Only a few girls at eleven and fourteen stake out their views on marriage versus career. Most are so family and romance oriented at this stage that they consider marriage only. The tasks in a counseling discussion might consist of enlarging their scope and encouraging self-evaluation, rather than focusing on career choice. (Description of Group Meeting is in Chapter 1.)

In general, the pre-adolescents are more homebound, father

[71]

attached, both resentful of yet closer to their mothers than the older girls. More than anything, the latter want to *get away* from their homes, while the former want both the hearth and the freedom. Friendships of both sexes serve as a form of security that they are recognized and accepted by others, hence are *real* and have an identity, however incomplete. These relationships replace those with parents and help in severing the tie.

The onset of menarche strengthens the turn to heterosexuality toward the end of early adolescence. This has taken place in all but one of the subjects. No longer supported by the internalizing of parental values, the older girls are thrown back to their own resources and seem to develop stronger convictions — the central fabric of identity formation. Attitudes toward occupational role are still indifferent and confused. At both ages, about a third have an almost superstitious, magical belief that a future career will spoil their chances of marrying, the be-all and end-all of their current conception of living.

# CHAPTER 5
## Pat: A Mid-adolescent at Age 18

Eighteen-year-old Pat is the eldest of four: a sister almost two years younger, and a brother and sister aged 10 and 8. When Pat was small, Mrs. O's younger sister lived with the family. Their present home is a pleasant single-family house with a lovely yard. Mr. O did considerable renovating himself, and his amateur paintings color the walls of the living room. The neighborhood is suburban; the schools rate well. Pat has attended the local school for only two years, enrolling when the family moved to their current home. Before that, they had lived in a rented apartment in a two-family house situated in a lower-middle-class section, more densely populated but retaining some rural areas. Pat attended a classical high school outside of the immediate neighborhood; it has a good reputation and high scholastic standards. Marked upward striving characterizes this family. They fall in the middle-middle level on the Hollingshead scale. There has been considerable stress, however, in the way of money and health problems.

*Background data*
Mrs. O, in her late thirties, is an attractive, trim, well-groomed woman. She uses words easily and selectively, stresses the amenities, and is quite controlled. One gets the impression that she edits her statements carefully. Tea was served as soon as the interviewer arrived.

The oldest girl and second eldest child in a family of six, Mrs. O grew up in a tumultuous, even tragic setting. Born in Ireland, both of her parents drank quite heavily; yet her father, a truck driver, managed to support them. Her mother, she says, was more interested in a good time than in caring for the children, — selfish and superficial. It was Mrs. O's assignment at an early age to take over for her mother — one that she resented bitterly. One day her mother went out with her friends, and the small brother Mrs. O was supposed to watch was killed in an accident. Just prior to Mrs. O's marriage, antagonism between mother and daughter flared and was openly expressed in a planned attack in which Mrs. O called her mother old and ugly, contrasting her with herself. It was after such an episode that her mother went out drinking and was killed in an accident. Mrs. O's reactions to these calamities were to pretend that things were different. "I would watch other people to see how they behaved." It was as if Mrs. O had no identity, so copied that of others in a rather primitive way.

Highly intelligent, Mrs. O attended a business college at night. She worked as a secretary for about five years, but did not enjoy it and has not worked since her marriage. Were she trained, she would like a job in a school or in research. Club life has little appeal although she and her husband do have a few friends and participate in church activities. She loves to read, especially historical novels.

Pat, according to mother, was a "perfectly average baby," walking and talking at the usual ages, ate well, enjoyed playing and was quite mischievous. "I don't recall anything out of the way. Yes, she had a good disposition, was quite lovable. I enjoyed her and still do. She has a fun-loving streak that appeals, was discerning and observant. In her early years, she did well in school; is the only one of the children who tells me what goes on there — which I enjoy. Pat liked bicycles, books and games, playing school, guessing games and tomboy activities, preferring boys as playmates. I think she was happier outside than in the house. She had one best friend at a time. The children played in mixed groups and boys thought of Pat as a pal. I don't want her to be coy and sweet, nor do I want her to be a pal. She

[74]

doesn't seem to know the things girls know — is too frank and aboveboard, leans too heavily on friends whose values I question."

Pat would make a fine teacher and a fine wife, Mrs. O believes. "But she tends to settle for second best — doesn't work hard enough, drifts, seems to scorn the intelligent type. I find this disquieting." It wasn't until last year that Pat mentioned career. Her mother feared that she might not want to go to college, which would have broken her heart. Pat, she feels, has a way with children, did well as a camp counselor. Nursing was wrong for her because "people get on her nerves, and she isn't giving enough. That and teaching are the two fields *we* had thought of. Her real ambition is to be a wife and mother. I tell her that even if she never teaches, the education will make her a better person. She'll probably have a large family — six. Since she was ten, she's been baby-sitting for me and is very responsible. In teaching, mothers often return to work later, and Pat may be able to do this. But there is nothing as important as bringing up a family."

The only truly stormy time with Pat was in the first year of high school. "She didn't want to study or do anything else. We just didn't get along. When she failed and had to repeat the year, there were many unpleasant, violent scenes." Mrs. O monitors and helps with homework, insists that Pat read the classics and go to summer school; she has arranged for Pat to attend outside courses. "If my children got all A's I'd have no problems." This statement is an oversimplification, however, because Mrs. O also deplores money limitations and daydreams of luxury cruises and exquisite clothes. A number of miscarriages, one witnessed by Pat, imposed strain.

Mrs. O wishes Pat had chosen a more demanding college, but "she doesn't have the will, is not an intellectual. I chide her on her lack of intellectual seeking — her absence of interest in politics. Her own self and her own affairs come first. I'd like to see her working with handicapped children — she's had a very

[75]

normal, average life, a good home, has never been deprived. Although she's had a religious training all her life and accepts the faith, she is not really devout." Mrs. O extols self-control.

Tall and handsome at forty, Mr. O looks worried, anxious and seems uncomfortable; he speaks in a well-nigh inaudible voice. Although he rarely looks at the interviewer, he seems sensitively aware of her presence, filling her teacup with alacrity.

Mr. O was brought up in the west, the second eldest of four, three boys and a girl. His father, who repaired machinery, was a brilliant man but erratic, and was away from home a great deal. Since their income waxed and waned, the family moved frequently, giving the children little chance to make friends; thus they had to stick together. "My father expected a good deal from us, but never showed us how." He died when Mr. O was 16. Mr. O's parents were both born in this country; his grandparents in Germany and Ireland. His mother was controlling and bossy — at times he thought of her as a cold, strange woman who had had a difficult life. Mr. O's older brother was her favorite and has never married. Father has seen his mother only once since his marriage.

Always bright, he was an extremely good student, editor of his school paper, and winner of a scholarship which he was unable to accept for financial reasons. He soon went into the army and was sent to Officers' Training School, taking courses in meteorology. Later he finished work for his degree in this field at night. He sometimes found it hard to exercise authority in supervising the technical phases of his job, where he spent many years. Now he has been transferred to a writing job in an industrial plant which he enjoys since he has long been interested in journalism. His health has been poor; he has been hospitalized at least twice for depression. Mr. O's illnesses were kept a family secret.

He described Pat as a bright child, quick mentally and physically. Things came a little too easily for her, so that whereas her work in grammar school had been excellent, she "met her match" later in a more difficult classical high school. As a baby, she proceeded according to a schedule, and learned easily, but she has always been a bit obstinate "like me she seemed to have a fairly tough rind."

She has "a little knack for drawing and writing, like me, and is quite creative. Pat, Mary and I formed a club for rhyming and guessing games. She had a lot of neighborhood friends. A little later around the eighth grade — she developed some embarrassment about her good ability in school, and toned it down so she wouldn't stand out."

Mr. O feels that nursing requires too much involvement with people for Pat who would, however, do well as a teacher. "She thinks more cerebrally, less emotionally. I think a person is pretty miserable if they are not working at capacity. Later when her children are at school, she will probably need something to fill her life, although it's a mistake to try to live two lives." Mr. O is disappointed at Pat's selection of a sectarian college, and fears she might meet some bigotry. She will keep her part-time job which she uses to earn money for trips and extras. Pat tends to hold back in declaring her decisions, "maybe because her mother has always made them for her."

Pat's sister Mary, 20 months younger than Pat, is a handicapped girl both emotionally and physically — the "ugly duckling" of the family. She has always functioned poorly in school, and gets into serious trouble in the neighborhood. Both are a source of great concern and an embarrassment to the family, especially to Mrs. O who stresses social facade. Her parents have sought and received professional help for Mary on a number of occasions. The two younger children are attractive and bright. John, the only boy, is a favorite with his father.

At 18 Pat is a tall, fresh-looking girl who resembles her father but whose looks, while attractive, suffer by comparison to her handsome mother. At first she seemed quite strained and flat;

[77]

later she became lively and humorous, especially when talking about school.

Her first comment: "I guess I always wanted to get married when I was a little girl and still do. Then, in the fifth grade, I wanted to be a teacher because I really liked that teacher; she always thought up new projects for us. I even remember kindergarten. We were allowed only two turns on the swings and I wanted it all the time. The first grade was more interesting — we colored pigs. In the second grade, there was a lot of drawing. I did a dog with his tail wagging and the teacher got mad and said, "you're not supposed to draw what you can't see." But I had it pretty good. She let me get up and tell the class stories I had made up. In the third grade, we had letters and made words, which was fun. As I said, the fifth grade really stands out but the next was boring. The teacher, a man, had no projects or anything. I never worked very hard." This is a recurrent theme.

Along with her parents, Pat chose the classical type of high school because the ones nearby were not very good and sent only a few graduates on to college. The first year in high school went well, although it was very demanding; after that she had trouble and had to repeat the eighth grade. "It was a bad year — I'm not a scholar. I like to read and do things, but Latin and math are not for me. There were hardly any clubs and the school was such a dark, dreary place, so formal and disciplined, and I missed seeing my friends because I didn't get home until five." When the family moved to the suburbs, a few years later, Pat transferred to the local schools which, in contrast, were far easier with lots of activities. "But my parents expected top grades. I guess because of my sister Mary's handicap they wanted me to be tops." Pat had an elective course in short-story writing and enjoyed it. "Physics was awful. My father is a whiz at it but I didn't ask him to help me because that makes me feel so stupid. Then he gets hurt because I don't ask." Senior year she wrote a

[78]

research paper on Graham Greene's *Search for God,* and received an A. Although Pat spent only two years at this school, she won a scholarship.

Actually Pat's memory reaches back to age 3 when she and Mr. O played ball. That was the first of many games with him and with her neighborhood friends, whom she mentions often. Mrs. O felt that she was not discriminating enough in these friendships. When Pat criticizes her mother, the words are mild but she flushes perceptibly. Pat was a leader, instigating many of the make-believe games which she loved. "Even before I was three, I remember driving back from the West when my father was discharged from the Army. I was happy that he would live with us now.

"Other games I remember included a rough game of house; the mother beat the children all the time and the father just watched. I never thought too much of being a nurse until the last few years. In the ninth grade, I got interested in hospitals and was fascinated by anything medical. But I worked in two hospitals after school and noticed that I felt depressed at the end of the week. I think it had something to do with the hospital, which had two floors closed; it was spooky and I had nightmares. Two of my friends who were student nurses said I'd get over it. They learned to accept death but I couldn't — I get too involved with people. Anyway, I didn't think I'd ever look as well in a uniform as they did. I can't stand serving people — even though I'm a waitress now. It would be better for me to be a teacher and serve minds instead of stomachs. Now I might like to be a teacher, but I'll leave the door open and change if it isn't right for me. I like children and get along with them, and teaching will give me a chance to keep learning. And there's always something new coming along. There will be new kids each year — a steady stream, sort of permanent.

"I still want to get married and teaching is practical for that. I wouldn't want to be anything but an elementary teacher; the

[79]

others don't seem to marry." Pat isn't too excited about college: It's sort of like going back to high school. It [the college she chose] is the best of the three tried. (The college is a fair sized, co-educational sectarian school to which she will commute.)

"I like writing children's stories and illustrating them. The one I did about my sister and brother pleased the teacher, who wanted me to send it to a publisher, but I didn't. Somehow I'd rather keep this a hobby. Other jobs I've thought of: teaching art or getting to be a guidance counselor." *Catcher in the Rye* is a current favorite; sometimes she imagines she is Holden Caulfield. Mostly Pat has been dating in groups in which the boys and girls may pair off and go to the movies later. Her current friend is a boy she has known for a long time. They work in the same place and tell each other their troubles. In the summer, when most of her friends are away, he takes her places. "I never used to like him, but now I do a little. He's not going to college and I doubt whether I'll know him next year. But he's a good kid."

"I don't want to sound boy-crazy, but I hope I'll be married ten years from now. I want to bring up my children, not always someone else's. But I wouldn't want to be a total housewife — I want to do something else too — writing stories or teaching sometimes. One thing I wouldn't do, and that is let a career interfere with marriage." Except for the effort her mother makes to influence her choice of friends, and take extra courses, Pat feels that she has made most of the decisions, although Mr. O disagrees. Mrs. O frequently asked why she didn't go around with "that nice girl or stay away from another. I think she's afraid I'll run off and marry some non-college man — and I would if I loved him, but I'd think about it first. I tend to like all kinds of people — even so-called cheap girls or girls who go to beautician school. I hate snobs."

Pat spoke of her diet and the Metrecal she had been taking.

[80]

This, she thought, was probably a placebo, adding "I don't trust anybody."

*Psychological test impressions of identity formation*

Pat is a bright, sensitive girl with a fertile imagination and a humorous, original twist to her perceptions. Her early and frequent references to clothes and parties underscore her concern with status and appearance and her love of pleasure.

One of the salient themes in her test responses is that of being forced by parents who, she feels, expect too much of her. This is especially marked by her perception of Mrs. O as a "domineering" mother, with whom identification seems intense but also ambivalent, for Pat is quite dependent on Mrs. O. In reaction, perhaps, Pat appears to "drag her feet," restricting her accomplishments, and giving more promise than she fulfills. She seems to equate achievement with spinsterhood protecting herself from that hated role, by restricting her accomplishments. Yet she wants to know and understand. There is a stronger-than-average identification with the role of the wife and mother in the TAT pictures, as well as with children. Identity is still somewhat immature but growing.

Pat is slow and wary in relating to people, making group rather than individual friendships. She may be reluctant to get involved for fear that she will lose them. It seems that she feels seriously disappointed in and let down by important people in her life; that family or foundations are emotionally charged and in danger is suggested by the Rorschach response "a tree with its roots and trunk on fire." TAT stories are quite transparent; she has little distance from some of the traumatic events of her life. One story deals with a man who has returned from an unexplained absence (father's return after hospitalization?). Such stories, together with the number of actual fatal accidents in the family, have undoubtedly left her with considerable foreboding

[81]

and apprehension over being destroyed, in retribution perhaps for her moments of rage.

Were she able to return to the world in nonhuman form she would *most* like to be (Pigem Test): "Sand — nothing can budge it. You would always be there, could never be destroyed and no one could hurt you. You could blow around in the desert." She would least like to be "a rattlesnake or something everyone would be on the lookout for so that you would eventually be killed." The choice of an inanimate identity in order to be permanent and safe suggests the extreme proportions of her fear of death. Yet Pat goes ahead with her plans despite the load of anxiety which disturbs her.

As a child, Pat tells us on tests she most admired her father; mothers are understanding but unkind. Fathers are also seen as watching but not protecting, and as "out of the picture"; she is aware of her father's second-class status in the home and cannot count on his support. Identification with him seems uncertain and clouded, yet he serves as a model for her in many ways. She most wanted to be like an aunt, about ten years older than she is, who used to live with them. Although Pat describes herself on the Sentence Completion as "happy-go-lucky," she feels "separated from her childhood," and compared with others, seems "backwards." A "laugh-clown-laugh" attitude prevails. The little girl in the TAT picture does not listen to the mother who is reading a story; she is thinking of something frightening that happened to her; she will never get over it.

Body image, as conveyed through a skillfully done, sharply delineated drawing of a girl her age features self-containment and intensity. The girl is highly feminine with a ballooning skirt, but is carefully controlled; her male drawing is a 19-year-old sailor without much ambition, who reminds Pat of the boy she is currently dating. As her ideal person, she draws a mother putting an infant to bed. Both mother and child have rather strained expressions, and the mother is holding the baby away

[82]

from her. Pat was the only subject in this study of 40 girls and women who drew both a mother and child, highlighting her preoccupation with marriage.

Through defenses of ego-restriction, avoidance, some repression, constructive use of fantasy and humor, Pat seems on the way to a more substantial identity. She recovers quickly from sudden angry primitive responses. Her perceptions do have a definite, clear-cut structure in most instances, and she backs them up with evidence. Both are identity components and bode well.

*Transactions among family members and Pat's identification patterns*

While the members of this family have considerable affection for each other, there are also negative currents which have shaped the identification pattern. Mr. O is critical of Mrs. O's inconsistency with the children, and feels that she makes them too dependent and runs their lives. Mrs. O's insistence on attendance at summer school, her monitoring of the children's homework and selection of what they must read, reinforces the impression of overcontrol. Moreover, she is a "back-seat" driver with Mr. O, making important decisions without consulting him — decisions which prevail. There is dissatisfaction with his income — "she talks poverty all the time." These criticisms are rarely expressed directly to his wife, for he is quite dependent on her and fears her icy withdrawal when criticized. But he refrains from expressing his anger. Of the same religious denomination as Mrs. O, his religious views are far less orthodox; there is a difference, too, in their socio-economic backgrounds, for his father was a skilled worker, hers drove a truck.

Mrs. O's image of her husband had been one of great strength; but when he needed hospital care, the picture changed. Her mother perceives Pat as "normal and average," while the predominant image held by father is one of brightness and creativity. Yet he has little tolerance for the children's quarrels, and the

[83]

chief bone of contention between him and Pat has been the fact that she does not spend enough time with Mary. Families should stick together, as his did. When Pat takes Mary with her, the latter's unwittingly deviant behavior results in embarrassment. Even more fundamental, Pat was aware of her mother's tragic experience when caring for her brother and this may have aroused anxiety in her when she was responsible for the younger children. She may ask herself: Will I destroy my brother as my mother did hers?

Mary's behavior, coupled with Mrs. O's high standards and expectations for Pat, her extreme reaction to Pat's one school failure, and the discrepancy between the views of the parents, all have created tensions. Pat is critical of some of Mrs. O's beliefs, resents her use of coercion and views her as "unkind." Yet she also admires and is dependent on her. Her identification with her mother seems quite ambivalent. Actually, she was given little opportunity to live as a child.

Until John was born, Pat was undoubtedly Mr. O's favorite. Is he the "little man with the big wings" Pat sees on the Rorschach? Mr. O formerly spent a good deal of time playing with her, but the playful father was no longer available when he was ill. Pat seems twice dethroned. He is the one she most admired as a child; her earliest memories center on him. Like Pat, he is a man with special sensibilities who empathizes with the needs and feelings of others. There is an identity of interests, traits and talents between them. But the relationship seems to have weakened somewhat, perhaps due to the disagreements about Mary and the "unexplained absence." (This is expressed chiefly in test reactions.) In delegating too much responsibility for the children to Pat, her mother set up a dubious model of femininity. She talks of the wonders of family life, but Mrs. O wants to rid herself of responsibility. Rather does she shift it to Pat and repeat her own childhood in demanding adult responsibility from a 10-year-old. Her precepts and behavior are at odds. It seems as if

[84]

Pat may have "caught" her mother's fears of violent death and feels fated to them. Her transient interest in nursing may have been an attempt to master these fears. And Pat has internalized some of Mrs. O's disparaging attitudes toward men.

Mrs. O's much younger sister, who lived with the family until Pat was 8, has since made a "good" marriage, and visits occasionally. She may play the role of big sister to Pat.

Pat's images of future work have run the gamut, but start and end with the role of wife and mother. The fifth-grade interest in teaching seemed to have revived during her senior year in high school and now prevails. Her strong emphasis on marriage has been reinforced by home and religious teaching and fanned by her mother's expressed opinions on marriage, as well as by her own desire to get away from home and her need for an emotional attachment. Pat seems to have strong peer identifications, often talking over her problems with friends in search of self-definition. An avid reader, she uses characters in books as identification figures, and like Holden Caulfield, she abhors the "phony."

*Ego development and journey through the stages*

Considering the strains rampant in this family shortly after Pat's birth, one might expect the growth of basic trust to be stunted somewhat in Pat as an infant. This was the time of Mr. O's hospitalization, Mrs. O's unwanted pregnancy with Mary followed by her birth and deviant development as well as Mrs. O's reaction to her mother's death. Mrs. O has never had a high degree of trust and is constantly warning Pat of sexual danger. Nor does Pat herself trust people. Mrs. O describes this early period as one of withdrawal and depression on her part; she may have been incapable of "giving" to the infant. Perhaps the arrival of the young aunt, then 13, supplied substitute mothering. Yet Pat does at times show a massive fear of being left and has a low degree of commitment, suggesting incomplete resolution of the tasks of this stage. In kindergarten, she wanted more

[85]

than she was given (turns on the swing). She is hungry for gratification in the form of clothes and status. Pat was probably allowed few choices in asserting her will and developing autonomy. Her ambivalence is quite marked.

In the initiative stage, Pat seems to have been a free-wheeling, investigative child with a rich fantasy life. She was both the possessive little girl and the tomboy who had more fun with boys than with girls. There was a definite turn to father and bisexual identification, the latter deriving from her aunt as well as Mrs. O. But the latter is often negative. Purpose and direction asserted themselves — the beginnings of a quite special little girl. A strong oedipal involvement with her father built up but appeared only in fantasy, that is, on tests. Her mother probably fostered the development of a precocious harsh conscience with concomitant guilt.

The industry stage is hard to evaluate. Pat did well in school until the eighth grade. She enjoyed projects and storytelling, was able to work well with others, wanted to be useful to teachers. Her failure in the eighth grade may have reflected the upset at home when her parents were involved in Mary's treatment and Mr. O was again hospitalized for depression; or to trouble in concentrating, to beginning adolescence and perhaps to the rigorous demands of the school itself as well as to Pat's general lack of involvement. This last trait may be more sporadic than diffuse, for Pat is not an inert girl. What sense of inferiority she has seems to stem from concern about status and appearance rather than ability. But as Pat herself says, she never works very hard. Her emphasis on popularity is more characteristic of the pre-adolescent than the mid-adolescent. She does not want to stand out as different from the group.

Now in mid-adolescence, Pat has settled on an occupational role. In narrowing her choice between nursing and teaching, she has been able to articulate her personal fears concerning the former, and some of the positives of the latter. Moreover, there

[86]

has been considerable clarification of her personal identity, sharper self-definition. She is beginning to wonder whether she really is the fat, happy-go-lucky, clownish servant that she visualized.

It is true that Pat seems lukewarm about teaching, too, but she does persist. Perhaps some of the strains of her life are reflected in a depressed point of view, which may also have been internalized from her father's dark moods. Both limit the degree to which she is able to mobilize commitment, whatever the phase of living. After her failure in the eighth grade, she rallied and managed to raise her grades and win a scholarship after only two years at the new high school. Should she achieve a fair degree of recognition in her work, her identity may solidify further. Rather than overidentifying, Pat appears to have made more partial and selective identifications, including those qualities germane to her own personal values.

The residual conflicts from her stormy voyage through the early stages may have been partially offset by the "tough rind." This does not mean that the rest of her life will be smooth sailing. But ego synthesis will benefit from an integration of healthy identifications and may be enhanced by an improved self-image. Pat has achieved some degree of differentiation from the values of her mother: the snobbery and emphasis on facade. Since she often suppresses her real feelings in talking of her family, the changing relationships with them is difficult to evaluate. And the discrepancy in parental viewpoints makes integration still more difficult.

Her ideas about marriage continue to be somewhat global and intense. There is more emphasis on her future children than on the differentiated qualities of her future husband. The latter may come after she has resolved further her oedipal involvement, although it is the task of mid-adolescence, and there has been some delay in completing the task.

Even after her children come, she has already decided to

[87]

maintain her freedom and be more than just a housewife. The boys she dates are perceived as pals, but her fears of sexuality have been accentuated since witnessing Mrs. O's miscarriages. While Pat's strongest commitment seems to be to her future family, she anticipates a dual or triple role. Gratification from success in her work and receiving recognition, plus the independence derived from being self-supporting, and a good marriage — all will probably bolster her identity further.

*Pat three years later*

Pat's appearance has not changed very much; she is a bit more slender and smartly dressed. She speaks of being tired due to the long trip to school and her part-time job as a clerical worker in a hospital. Early in the talk, she mentions her plan to be a student teacher next semester. "I'm looking forward to it more than I thought I would, but I'm still a little luke-warm. I'm not devoted to it but I think I'll enjoy it anyway. And college has been fun, not too hard. I mean I haven't done exceptionally well and yet I haven't really worked hard." Her grade average is 82 or a B, but it would not have been difficult to do exceptionally well. "I'm in all those methods courses you just take for credits because you don't really learn very much. They are so dull. I'm majoring in English and toying with the idea of going to grad school in English. I may right after graduation or I may wait. Most of our courses are liberal arts and that's why I think it's a good school. We have to take theology and philosophy, but I have taken all my other electives in English.

"I've scraped and saved and worked while going to school for so long that I'd like a free period where I can buy what I want and travel." Theology rather than religion is stressed at college, the scientific, dramatic elements. "I think I've become more intellectual about my religion, but a lot of the students are bigots because they've had nothing but parochial schools and they can't think. I can't say my faith has been reinforced because

[88]

I resent a lot of what they say but you can't argue, neither do you accept things blindly. Insofar as a range of philosophers go, even Plato is refuted in favor of the ones who fit the doctrine. They're not objective. Actually my father didn't want me to go to this college because of the bigots here. Contrasted with my mother's religious beliefs, mine and his tend to be sort of easygoing and tolerant."

No, she has not been able to take any courses in the writing of children's stories, although she has always wanted to. "If it were pressing I would, but I generally don't do things unless they are. And I don't like reading things I've written out loud. I've had fun all the time — doing a lot of things — I think I *found myself* more in college. I'm reasonably popular, more so than in high school. Then I was popular with individuals but now I'm popular with the class in general. I ran for class vice-president and lost by only five votes, but it didn't bother me. I stopped smiling at all the people I didn't like. There was a time when I never would have thought of running.

"Sometimes I think I've become more shallow because I don't seem to care about my school work whereas I used to worry — that I wasn't 'living up to your potential' as my mother says; yet I am not losing any sleep about it. While I'm clever, I'm not really a student. I love reading but not studying. When something really catches my interest, I work — like in English. Some of the hard-working students are perfectionists, but my father is one and I don't want to be. He really can make himself unhappy with it, though he's very intelligent. He has this drive that I lack — both my parents do. They aren't as upset about this any more and don't nag the way they did formerly. Occasionally they'll say: 'Don't you ever study?' " By and large, Pat characteristically tones this down by adding "I'm not home much." She supposes she is happy at home, even though she would rather live in the dorms. Mrs. O is now working as a secretary part-time and keeps quite busy.

[89]

Pat has no regret about giving up nursing. When she was a freshman at college she took Interest Tests and the counselor tried to convince her that she belonged in the nursing course, but she disagreed. "At the end of freshman year, I was a little fed up and thought about going to an out-of-town university, but I'm glad I stayed because I got to know everybody, and now I feel a loyalty to the school that I didn't have then."

Asked for her conception of teaching, Pat said that you have to be ready for the unexpected; there are always different levels for different children. "But I don't think much about the subject matter, I just think of the children but I have to force myself to think of the stuff I have to teach them. I think of the little bossy girl who will be reporting on everybody and the little child who is just plodding along, and how I'll help them. Not that you can devote all of your time to their problems because you have to teach them things. I think of a nice classroom, and I'd never want the kids to be afraid of me as I was of my teachers, but I don't want kids running all over the place. The big thing is to love reading — that would be my scholastic aim for them. My chief aim would be to build a sense of their own words. That would carry them through a lot of other things. I know I couldn't do it with all of them."

In discussing models that she used in growing up, Pat thought that around the fifth grade she was copying Nancy Drew and other characters in books because "I was a tomboy then and went around drumming up trouble like Nancy." (She is the character who helps a great detective, and could be a father figure.) "Actually I don't think I ever tended to copy either parent ever, unless I did it subconsciously. I may have put on their clothes once, but I never played house to any degree and don't have the image of the housewife like my mother anyway, although it's hard to categorize her, she's so diversified.

"My old friends and I have gone our separate ways. Most of them didn't go on to college. There was one girl I was close to in high school, but we've grown apart. She has no authentic personality of her own, and was sort of my foil — I made all the decisions. I like people who know their own minds and contribute. There's no special boy in my life, but I go out a lot — I just haven't met anyone really interesting or maybe I'm too fussy.

"Maybe my aunt had a big-sister image for me. I liked her sense of humor and her intelligence and she too was a reader. She has four children and a husband who is quite dramatic but rock steady, while she's a little flighty. She was the one who took us out for special occasions, like a grandmother, and no one else did; we don't have many relatives.

"My mother's cousin is married to a man I really admire. If I marry anyone, that will be my type. He's a great big red-haired type — a sailor during the war. After that he went to law school and has been studying for years and finally passed the bar, despite having a large family. He likes me, too, and is a great kidder."

In general, Pat feels more free and independent. Looking ahead ten years, she doesn't want to be left on the shelf. But it does not make her panic now. "This drives my mother crazy. A lot of my friends are engaged and she wonders why I can't see something in some of the kids, *but I'd never marry just to get married.* In ten years I hope I am because I want a lot of children and to be young and energetic with them. If I do, I'd never be tied to the house or do more than I have to. I would never make housework my life. I'll get sitters — find the money somewhere. Probably I'll go back to teaching when the children are in junior high. I'm interested in politics too, and I'd like to do something worthwhile as well as to have fun — groups and clubs and things. But there might not be time, what with the children, for all of these things." Pat hopes to have five children, but may settle for three. "Maybe after one, I'd be too tired for more. There are things you can do to help keep your sanity. If you want to make time, you can. If you thought you were about to go off the deep end, you'd have to get out even though the house wouldn't be so clean." Pat would like to marry a very intelligent man so that they could enjoy reading, not the kind that you have to meet at the door with a pie. But if he wanted her home, she feels, she would have to be subservient to some extent. But then she'd have a "darn good time at home, and have all my meetings there."

At the close of the talk, Pat speaks rather reticently about her concern with her looks and her crooked teeth. "It really bothers me. Really it bothers my mother more — she keeps saying 'Why didn't I ever have Pat's teeth straightened?' I know I've never been particularly pretty, but maybe I'll wear well. It isn't as bad now as it was." Pat recognized that these feelings vary with her moods.

At 21, the phase of later adolescence in which consolidation and clarification of one's way of life takes place, Pat has made considerable progress. She knows herself better, has found herself at college, and has taken real strides in self-esteem. Her earlier sense of inhibition and conventionality have shifted to freedom in expressing her individuality; she has firmer convictions and admires people who know what they believe in. Her vistas have expanded, and now include such wider aspects of life as politics. Currently she feels loyalty to her college — the fidelity which had not shown its face earlier. In college, she has made a try for an important leadership role. But Pat's self-image still has a negative quality: her feeling of being unattractive. Apparently her mother must have perfection in her children.

Not only has she settled on a profession, the task which Erikson (1963) places at the heart of the identity crises in late adolescence, but she is looking forward to the induction stage just ahead. Moreover, she has found the specialty within teaching which truly excites her: English. Her statement that she works hard at what she likes augurs well. And her conception of the

[92]

aims and criteria of the "good teacher" seem mature, even perspicacious. Limits on her commitment still persist as does the sizable strand of pleasure-seeking in her life, which reaches even to the time when she has children. Her refusal to be "tied down" endures. The weak investment which seems to pervade Pat's life might also derive from her massive anxiety regarding death. Were she to allow herself to become truly involved with life she might suffer its loss.

Her former frenetic attitudes toward marriage have modulated. The role of mother superordinates that of wife. Her male ideal is the achieving, virile, intelligent man, her cousin. Her teeth are not a negative feature of serious import. Mrs. O's part-time job is probably diluting her concern with Pat, while the young aunt has contributed the supportive feeling of having a relative who played the giving role. There has been some resolution of the triangular situation, resulting in part from Pat's improved relationship with her mother, and her sharing of intellectual and religious values with her father. But the ambivalence of her feelings precludes genuine identification. Pat's functioning is especially impressive when viewed in the light of the strains in her life while she was growing up.

*Interpenetration of identity formation and occupational role: work psychodynamic*

Pat perceives herself as a reader, but not a student. It is this love of reading that she wants to communicate to her pupils. Both in her fun-loving and in her intense fears, she identifies strongly with children. This should help her empathize and achieve effectiveness with them. Her choice also meshes with her dependency which she covers up in the interview but not in the projective tests.

Perhaps identification with her teachers, especially with the one in the fifth grade, partially motivated her choice. In the teaching role she will have latitude for expressing her performing

[93]

needs as well as her creativity and leadership qualities. On a more manifest level, Pat visualizes teaching as a continuous and therefore satisfying learning situation. Until her bad experience at the classical high school she was happier in school than she was at home. Teaching may be a way of perpetuating such an environment. It is also the profession both parents favored for her.

Pat counts on a return to teaching after marriage, partially, she says, to keep her "from going off the deep end," and again, "to maintain her sanity." She may be wondering whether she, too, is like her father in having poor emotional health, or whether she may develop some of Mary's deviations.

Applying the Blos formulation, we might infer that the operating principle in Pat's choice reflects the unresolved conflicts in the earlier stages of childhood — her marked fear of being left and deserted. An effort to actively master the trauma of this period through the repetition compulsion propelled her toward an occupation in the nurturant grouping for which she has an affinity. Her anxiety about the imminence of sudden death and the longing for permanency in life are related to her choice of what she would most like to be were she to return to the world. "Sand because it would always be there." So, too, would there be a sort of permanence or continuity in the choice of teaching because of the "steady stream" of children entering school year after year. The school may symbolize a safe cloister from her fears, as well as the habitat of perpetual youth. If so, Pat's occupational role by serving as a means of externalizing her conflicts may reinforce some of the positive aspects in her identity. This in turn may reverberate to added competence in performing her occupational role, based on the reciprocal interchange between the two entities which tie together the unity of the ego. The process of ego synthesis has been on-going; she has greater self-esteem. Acceptance of herself as she is lags somewhat, but despite this, her urge to master problems is strong. Nor would she marry anyone just to be married.

*Blind comparison of 1964 and 1967 projective test records*

A striking degree of maturation has taken place in Pat between 1964 and 1967. She has considerable capacity for creative and original activity, which was appreciably blocked in 1964 by her passivity and her defensive orientation toward conformity. At that time she was consequently unproductive. An underlying depression fed into the traits of passivity and dependency. Hopeful zest in undertaking new tasks was lacking, and gratifications were relatively few. By 1967 passivity and pessimism have decreased and Pat's willingness and ability to experiment with new approaches, ideas and experiences have increased.

In 1964 the developmental tasks Pat was dealing with seemed more typical of Erikson's "school age," or early rather than mid-adolescence. The issue of industry versus inferiority was foremost. Pat was deeply involved with the question of acceptance by her peers. Her major interest was her own personal appearance, centering around clothes, grooming and having fun. By contrast, in 1967 she judged herself and others more in terms of personality traits and less on the basis of appearance and "popularity." Character traits like honesty, thrift, intelligence and persistence have become important. Her attitude toward work changed from its being just "a relief" when a hard task was completed to "a satisfaction." Her wish to be married continued but with more recognition of the *wife* role as well as that of the mother.

A major cause of her progress in the identity search seems allied to the great change in her perception of men and women. In 1964 she saw women as powerful decision-makers who controlled men and children, often arbitrarily. They were wiser than men. Men were seen as kind but ineffectual and generally "out of sight," and boys seemed like irresponsible children to her, fun-loving and unruly. (An expressed disdain for boys covered

[95]

a strong wish for them to like her and nervousness in their presence.) By 1967, women began to appear more human to Pat, and often vulnerable. The basis of these changes seems to be a better resolution of her ambivalence toward Mrs. O. In 1964, she consciously expressed admiration and respect for her, while her projective material showed intense rage at her and a wish for rebellion and revenge. By 1967 much of this conflict had become conscious and hence caused less disruption of activity. Pat no longer needed to insist on her mother's adequacy to all situations, and was better able to tolerate her anger at her mother. This helped her to see Mrs. O more realistically as having both faults and strengths, and to give up the exaggerated identification with her mother and seek her *own* unique identity. At the same time Pat became able to value certain traits she had previously considered masculine, particularly intellectual achievement and a vocation.

At 21, she took a more serious approach and acknowledged the importance of one's beliefs. She felt her own had stability. This change typifies one of the major shifts in her whole orientation to life, seen in *many* areas, a shift away from escapism and avoidance of problems to a more direct confrontation of issues and active attempts at solution. In her drawings, for example, both 1964 figures are "just standing." In 1967 the both figures are engaged in an appropriate activity.

In 1964 Pat's sense of identity was fluid and uncertain and she dealt with the anxiety aroused by this uncertainty through an exaggerated and premature adoption of a borrowed identity closely resembling certain qualities of her mother. There was virtually no willingness to experiment with different roles. The life of the young housewife and mother was seen as the idyllic solution to all problems. Motherhood was perceived as an ideal combination of security, power and gratification. The role of the husband in the family was shadowy and of negligible importance. The amount of work involved in this career was grossly

[96]

underestimated. Hints of some interest in a job outside the home were present, but these were vague and weak.

By contrast, in 1967 Pat was grappling with establishing an identity of her *own* and experiencing more conscious awareness of various real possibilities. *She expressed more interest in becoming a teacher and believed that she could be a good one,* "with persistence." Her 19-year-old focus on externals and appearances shifted to broader feminine interests. [For example, her 1964 preoccupation with clothing and decoration by 1967 had become less centered on her own personal adornment.] She had developed a general interest in beauty which included aesthetic appreciation of larger segments of the environment, such as lovely scenery or art objects. She gave up the teenage comic strip stereotype of being pretty and popular, soon to be a glowing young bride. Instead, she began to acknowledge some of her own needs to know, learn, and have a sense of individual accomplishment.

Perhaps she is not yet ready to endanger her emerging identity by the kind of closeness which she fears would be engulfing. Because of her reluctance concerning intimacy, one would speculate that, in spite of the theme of early marriage in the 1964 record, Pat will marry at an average or late time compared with other college women.

There has been important progress in ego synthesis over this period. In 1964, Pat was afraid of the explosiveness of her emotional reactions. When deep impulses reached awareness she experienced them as alien and frightening. By 1967, emotion and thought had been integrated remarkably well.

Successes seemed to have decreased her depressive feelings, and this change also led to greater freedom. In 1964 there had been considerable conflict between her urges toward original, creative thought and her wish to remain a passive conformist in order to satisfy dependency needs. In 1967, independence was no longer seen as so dangerous, and trial-and-error seeking be-

[97]

havior was replacing conformity and pain-avoidance tactics. Her self-image had changed from an inferior, explosively hostile person trying in vain to emulate idealized others to a potentially productive, self-actualizing adult. Her fears seemed much less intense than formerly.

By 1967, Pat had bolstered her repression of infantile urges and was able to manage immediate problems by more advanced techniques, especially rationalization, humor and intellectualization.

JEANNE F. GRIFFEN, PH.D.
*Clinical Psychologist*

*Follow-up information*

I spoke with Pat in 1972. She had been teaching sixth grade in an all-black school in a section of the city where there has been racial trouble. But she had not experienced any difficulty, she said, and really enjoyed the children, many of whom were culturally retarded. She has always wanted to travel, however, and has applied for a job teaching the children of men overseas.

"You are probably surprised that I am not married — I talked so much about it. But I haven't met the right man and my mother thinks I'm too fussy. I date an average amount, even tried the Computer Dating Plan and met some interesting men, but they were from out of town mostly. There are men teachers in my school, but they are not my dish of tea. I really enjoy the children but not the detail work. Now that I'm working and have a car, I'm pretty free, go skiing most weekends." Pat is still working toward her master's degree at night.

The other new development is that she is having her teeth straightened. "It's expensive and I hope it will be worth it. Anyway it will please my mother."

[98]

# CHAPTER 6
## Developmental Progress of the Group
## of Mid-adolescents

This report presents another overview, this time of the group of high school seniors at two developmental stages; and contrasts the regularities within each stage (Groups I and II). Mostly eighteen when we met for the first time, they returned at age twenty or twenty-one. The emphasis herein is on comparing the developmental progress at mid- and late adolescence with those of the younger girls.

On the Hollingshead Scale, the families have been classified as predominately middle-middle social class with a scattering of upper- and lower-middle features; they are notably upward-striving.

Almost half of the parents' parents were born in Europe (a larger proportion than in the preceding group). Both sets of families own their homes which are often fairly new and sub-stantial. Mothers have a better than average education, com-parable with those in Group I; two earning advanced degrees, two doctorates, whereas most fathers have finished a four-year college program, while only a few did graduate work. They grew up in the Depression, emphasize the value of security, de-plore their daughters' naivete with money. These men do quite well at work. There are more professional fathers and somewhat fewer men in business. Some of the girls have expressed an oc-casional desire to go into business with their fathers, later with their husbands.

Intelligent as a group, mothers give the impression of tension and strong drive. They are convinced that sufficient will is the cornerstone of success. A few are still active in their professions,

[99]

a physician and a teacher. They seem genuinely concerned about what to do with their time now that their children will be away at college. A few spoke of a friend in a similar position who had started to drink heavily; one mother was alcoholic, almost a third spend inordinate amounts of time cleaning their homes. To a striking degree, they extol education: "If my child were doing well in school, I would have no problems." Private lessons in dancing, music, art, and even charm are on their daughters' bulging agendas. Parents, it seems, identify with their children as children do with them; also identify them with aunts, uncles, or other relatives with whom they are using the child to fight old battles.

It is generally accepted that the daughters will go on to college. In a few instances, they have been steered and even pushed in the direction of a field which the parent (usually mother) wanted but did not achieve, often a prestigious field. A few girls play the role of a girl friend rather than daughter; mothers find it hard to let them grow. Actually mothers seem overinvested. Slightly more than half are not "tuned in" to daughters' network; and restrict their participation in decision-making. Moreover, social pressures accent mothers' ambitions for prestige colleges and occupations as does competition with family members. Brothers were sent to the Ivy League colleges and had priority over sisters' educations, leaving resentment and jealousy in their wake.

Perspective and understanding of the usual rebellion and antagonism of early and mid-adolescence is expressed by almost a third of the mothers. Some of the others reacted intermittently with puzzlement or anger and irritation. There was wrangling over what mothers regard as insufficient studying and "poor" performance which is actually fairly "good," as well as indecision about future occupation and clothes. This disapproval comes at a time when the girl is expressing general antagonism and rebellion toward the mother, exacerbating the impact on her. In

[100]

late adolescence, however, the quarreling has moderated considerably. But disagreement about dating and going steady persists, perhaps to a more moderate degree.

Most mothers believe their daughters could handle a combination of marriage and career. Almost half of them appear to have shortages in their role as identification figures, so preoccupied are they with their own imperious needs, while the rest tend to support growth. There is, however, a small strand of out-and-out antagonism to the idea of women working at all. Whether or not their own mothers worked along with individual religious affiliation seems associated with this dichotomy, the former group tending to reject the dual track when their mothers were employed after marriage.

Fathers expressed more positive attitudes toward daughters, insisting, however, that fathers are poor informants, that mothers know daughters better because fathers are away a lot and busy when at home. This is actually true to a striking degree; it is a prominent group characteristic, encompassing more than half of the group. The girls feel this separation keenly, view it as both physical and psychological separation. "My father does not know me. I wish I knew what he thinks and expects of me." Though this also happens with Group I girls, it is less prominent there. Is father away because of expediency or is he excessively absorbed in business or does the absence reflect disappointment with the marriage?

The calibre of communication between the parents seems low. Father's absence from the home isolates mother socially, and this may be reflected in the quality of the mothering.

In families consisting of two girls, father generally favors the older one, who is frequently a good athlete. Though fathers approve mildly of daughters' plans to work after marriage, they limit it to earning the money that the daughter may need should something happen to her husband — as in Group I. Mothers are

[101]

genuinely more ambitious than fathers for their daughters' success at work.

For older brothers, feelings run strong and deep. It is interesting that the brothers are decisively and openly their mothers' favorites. As one might expect, fathers were generally antagonistic about this and turned even more to their daughters, encouraging them to play the sons' roles. But three years later these mid-adolescent identifications with brothers had usually become diluted, especially when the latter had married or were living away from home.

That mothers appear to be the dominant parent may have grown partly out of necessity because fathers are away. Which came first is hard to know.

*Identification patterns*

Communication and relationships between the girls and their mothers were generally at low ebb at this period but revived somewhat in late adolescence. Predominantly negative or ambivalent identifications with mothers prevail. These antagonisms are manifested primarily in projective test data; only slightly more than a third spoke of them in the interview. Many identify with either or both parents in varying ways; it is not an all or none phenomenon. But there is a clear-cut strength to the father attachments at this stage, a pattern reflecting partially the currently active but incomplete attempt at resolving the oedipal involvement. The struggle seems less intense and closer to resolution when the girls returned at age 20 to 21, paralleling improvement in relationships with mothers. This is a vital dynamic. Erikson says. "This revived oedipal struggle is not . . . exclusively even primarily a sexual one; it is *a turn toward the earliest origins,* an attempt to resolve a diffusion of early introjects, and to rebuild shaky childhood identifications."

In contradistinction to the boy, Blos describes the girl as continuing "to spin the oedipal tapestry all through latency. The

[102]

polarity of fixity in 'masculine' or 'feminine' receives its final form at mid-adolescence."

A second task is the move toward disengagement from early ties, a step in the evolving of their own identities. She is usually able to accept her heterosexuality, and to learn to evaluate men more realistically. More than half seemed unsuccessful in disentangling triangular snarls and still had mixed, predominantly hostile identifications with mothers. The mixture of love and hate which teems in this group appears to be a replica of feelings in early childhood. Most of the girls seek substitute identification figures in further effort to break away from parents. Peer models constitute the bulk of these. The core of self grows as the girls build their own convictions, preferences, loyalties and values, and especially awareness and acceptance of selves.

More than half of the girls show a lingering strain of bisexuality. A definite masculine coloring or a forced feminine one or considerable sex role confusion plagues. Despite this residual, at late adolescence it seems to have moderated considerably. While a few disparage marriage, all plan it as an eventual way of life, but plan to delay it until after some years of occupational activity. But mid-adolescence is the first stage where the girls tolerate the plan of both family and career — the double track. About half of the subjects place marriage at the very center of existence, showing a strong need for an emotional attachment.

It is interesting that there is a slight trend for the children who played games such as school to become teachers, the pretenders to select art or dramatics while the make-believe nurse actually decided on this profession. Children may tend to sustain strong interests; there may be some parallelism between play and future work. The seniors want to be helpful and work in a group. Part-time or summer jobs helped them to know themselves better and experiment with roles, as they did in the vocational clubs in high school. There are strong identifications with teachers, camp counselors and club leaders in general.

[103]

*School and projective test reactions*

Some of the seniors had spent their entire school lives in the same system and the cumulative reports go back to kindergarten. A perceptive teacher will occasionally comment on behavior which presages quite accurately a current characteristic of the student. A few girls made poor records; school was a strain from the beginning and caused severe discord with parents who were forcing on their daughters work which was beyond them academically. Stress also marked the freshman year at college for pupils who were considered excellent students in high school. This resulted in curriculum shifts and new goals. Two girls transferred out of pre-medical courses because the math was too difficult, despite advanced courses in high school. Perhaps the transition from secondary school to college could be smoothed through use of counseling. A few seniors had no idea about goals or vacillated. This seemed to trouble them, confirming Erikson's statement that "it is primarily the inability to settle on an occupation which disturbs young people." When they returned three years later, there were two more prospective teachers who implemented their plans, as did the nurse, and also one who specialized in merchandising. One switched to a major in history of art; another decided to major in psychology and eventually work at it in her father's business. But she had quite a struggle to complete college and was refused admission to graduate school, while one who is extremely bright, flunked out of college, and now wants to teach the dance or do choreography. Currently she is back at college in response to her mother's urging.

If by senior year at college, uncertainty about a role still reigns, or no broad direction exists, a more pervasive disorder might be suspected. Sometimes teaching is selected primarily because it fits into a shorter and more flexible work schedule.

On psychological tests, more than half of the girls respond with indications of high intelligence and fanciful activity. The latter revolves around stories of "hideaways" or "freedom rides"

[104]

where they can do anything they want, sheer expression of impulse. Many of their test responses deal with "dehumanized leprechauns and gremlins" — suggesting a childlike weakness of perception but also a lively one. There is a collision between the pleasure-loving side and that bound by duty and conscience which might be expected at 17 or 18 when instinctual life is proliferating. Men are often viewed as sexually dangerous: "An ape coming toward me," a typical response at this age. The imaginative quality has slackened off when the girls returned at around age 20 and demonstrated a tighter control by the defenses; perception of reality had also improved. Themes of cheating and stealing are less prominent in this group and there was a more disguised anger. At mid-adolescence, it is clear that they resent being forced by parents, especially mothers, who have disappeared or died. This too has tempered later. Worries about death, about being "stuck," or "left on the shelf" — all are conspicuous themes. As may be expected, egocentricity is quite pervasive as attachment is drawn away from parents. A good deal of the above, however, suggests an identity which has grown.

*What seems to be going on with the mid-adolescents?* A struggle for self knowledge, acceptance, realistic self-esteem; for showing what they can do as persons and for the receipt of group approval as a result; for the channeling of beginning goals as a precursor to staking out larger units of the kind of life they truly want, be it predominantly marriage and children, or career, or both. The striving for autonomy looms large, as does the urge to differentiate self from parents. The girls reach for new experiences; they try to relax early attachments while substituting others; and they come to terms with a fixed sex role based on an improved identification with mothers and a compromise but resolved romance situation with fathers. They want more understanding between the generations, especially in teenage mores and specificity about the ground rules in their

[105]

dates with boys, for a new date galvanizes them. They want equal status with siblings in their parents' hearts, friends of both sexes, group identifications. But more than anything they want authenticity and consistency between what parents do and what they say. The girls abhor "phonies," they want parents to be realistic and dependable.

Most of the above can be applied too in building an occupational identity. The majority strive hard to grow up, but a few have moments of clinging to childhood; this too is a universal experience of the frightened individual, one from which she usually recovers when adequately supported for a period.

At 20 or 21 when they returned for a second evaluation the girls answered the "Who am I?" question with "This is me," expressing more certainty about the kind of person they are and want to be. The consolidation process which looms so important at the stage of late adolescence makes itself felt in more stable, predictable behavior, fewer mood swings, and greater purpose and direction as well as a larger capacity to compromise and tolerate delay of impulses. The mid-adolescents show a distinct advance in abstract thinking over the early adolescents while resentment for mother gradually decreases. On the other hand, spontaneity and creativity have decreased and some characteristics have jelled to a greater extent.

As the girls talked about their majors and other college activities or their jobs, one was impressed with the extent to which they have put the stamp of their individuality onto their future careers which are indeed personally determined. By studying aspects of the repetition compulsion, a congruent interpenetration of identity and occupation can be tentatively traced and synthesized from the wealth of data available and used systematically.

*The ego in adolescence*
In adolescence, mid and late, it would seem that the ego is

recovering from its relative impoverishment in early adolescence when the pressures of puberty leave their mark. It is apparently not unusual for the girl who has been able to handle strains previously to react to early and beginning adolescence with extreme tension. This is sometimes exacerbated by parental attitudes of disapproval and restriction at this time when parents also become tense in reaction to their daughters' sexual maturity and belligerent independence and defiance. This may reach back to their own uncertainty at a similar period in their lives. Blos (1963) and Infelder and Piaget (1958) make the point that instinctual drive organization and ego development go hand in hand; that effective growing up and progress in cognition correlate to a high degree. The adolescent moves from egocentricity to decentering which promotes objectivity.

As the girl in mid-adolescence loosens her early parental ties in an effort to differentiate herself, she also loses the support of the super-ego or conscience derived from internalizing parental values which are now rejected. The model is: "I love what I would like to be." Transient identifications of mid-adolescence also contribute equilibrium, as does the frenetic activity germane to the stage interpreted by Blos (1963) as outlets for social hunger counteracting feelings of loneliness over losses and changes in relationships. Difficulty in handling love and hostility for the same person reaches its apex in this stage. But most girls function, and the effectence motivation of White (1959) is clearly visible.

Seven of the ten girls in Group II (mid-adolescents) are now married. More than half work as secretaries while their husbands do graduate work. Only a teacher, two nurses, and a scientist have been fairly constant in carrying out the tentative plans they had in high school. One is still undecided; another who is probably the brightest in the group now married, returned to college at her mother's behest after the student gained too much weight to continue dancing, in which she had lost interest.

[107]

The choice of vocation — whether it is architecture or motherhood, requires the relegation of some ego models, ego ideals, possible selves — to subordinate positions, for mid-adolescence is the stage during which these ranking processes are initiated. It is during late adolescence that they assume a definite structure. The student begins to think of the future and considers himself the equal of the adult. Mid-adolescence seems to come to an end, Blos suggests, when late adolescence is ready to be transformed into young adulthood or post-adolescence through a thrust of the task of consolidation which results in a more unified ego with stable expressions through love, work, and ideology. And stabilized self-esteem is one of cardinal achievements of childhood. But late adolescence is also a crisis period with both Blos and Erikson. It taxes the integrative capacity of the individual, and can result in delays in development. As Freud said "Work has a greater effect than any other technique of living in the direction of binding the individual more closely to reality . . . . [It] provides for a considerable discharge of libidinal impulses, narcissistic and aggressive, and even erotic; then it is indispensable for subsistence and justifies existence in a society."

In mid-adolescence (around 18) there is more stability and solidity to the pattern of behavior. It features open antagonism for mother figures and increased positive feelings for fathers. The latter endures into late adolescence, but in a milder form. Then consolidation is the phase-specific task; there is greater purpose and direction plus a more unified ego.

Those identifications which shore up and mature identity seem to be the selective, discriminating, and largely positive ones, chosen partly because of their affinity for the subject's *own* ideology. When the integration of identifications squares with the central ideology of the girl herself, it grows rapidly, drawing water as a plant does when it chooses the needed elements from the atmosphere. This centrality which ideally invades and pervades the individual etches its personal and private signature

[108]

both on the emerging identity and on the choice of occupation.

Mid-adolescence (17 or 18) is the stage of the diary or journal, important as the thrust of activity reverses itself in the direction of greater passivity and awareness. Now there is even a stronger turn toward heterosexuality, and this helps in the resolving of the oedipal attachment which is one of the main tasks of this stage. Mother is the fallen idol, but feelings for father are still largely positive. With work at college still ahead, choices become more enduring.

Now the girl breaks away from early parental ties with less anxiety. There is a definite swing toward boys; she has the capacity for tender love at this point of development. But such feelings like most are charged with ambivalence. Narcissistic feelings abound; the girl tends to overvalue herself.

The girls express interest in religion and in self-discovery. There is an exquisite intensity of feeling, and heightened sensibility amounting almost to depersonalization.

Three years later found the same girls at the stage of *late adolescence* characterized by consolidation and integration — the calm after the storm of mid-adolescence. Emotions are now more constant and self-esteem has risen so that sense of self is clearly delineated.

Under the general aegis of the exploratory process, our *mid-* and *late adolescents* are in the transition stage of choice. Reality considerations are now given more weight as girls either enter the employment market or go on for additional training. Some had implemented their choice by starting nurse's training or enrolling in a school of education. Others linger at a process used in an earlier period and characterized by doubt and uncertainty. More than one out of four crystallized a choice and were in the trial stage of an occupation.

[109]

# CHAPTER 7
## Mrs. V: A Young Adult with a Pioneer Identity

A small, energetic woman of 27, Mrs. V radiates self-assurance, optimism, and animation. Her manner is breezy and forthright; her colorful conversation peppered with superlatives, humor, slang, and four-letter words. Highly intelligent, alert and vital, she openly expresses her contempt for stupidity, and lack of awareness and dullness in others.

Mrs. V is married to a scientist and now works as a free-lance technical writer, composing, designing and producing instruction manuals for operating complicated machinery. She also prepares highly scientific research reports for publication, editing the texts as well as supervising layout, typography and illustration. With considerable enthusiasm, she proudly displayed a sample of her work to the interviewer.

Mrs. V finds her job stimulating, especially enjoys doing it on a free-lance basis. "If I want to stay home and paint my house, I can do it. I can take time off while illustrations are being prepared." She works best under pressure. "Writing is a hard job. It takes discipline and sweat, and I can't do it unless somebody wants it yesterday." There is a lot of preliminary work needed. "I want to know, for instance, exactly how a machine works, what makes it tick." In addition to reading all available material about a machine, she examines it, operates it, questions the man who invented or operates it, predicts the pitfalls a new operator might experience.

At college she majored in sociology and anthropology; then, after an interval of one year, went on to graduate work in journalism. This included a course in technical writing. "That gave you an idea about it, although it's not really adequate preparation. But the knack for this work can be developed if you have a feeling for language and for things mechanical and scientific. I'm of the opinion that editors are born and not made. I've always written and love words." For the most part, however, her training came on the job, and she received further help and encouragement from her husband. "I never was really interested in the sciences, except in a general way, but my husband makes it all so fascinating, and he has a wonderful way of explaining things clearly." Her first technical writing job came through her husband, who helped her design a brochure for the engineering company where he works. Later she was called in to edit a technical manuscript and thereafter, a steady stream of jobs came her way.

"This was something I'm interested in and can make money on. After all, nobody is going to pay me to write the great American novel." She knew, too, that she was not likely to get ahead in anthropology, her major — "unless I go on to get a Ph.D. in the subject and trot off to a Navajo reservation. Besides," says Mrs. V, "to make money, you go into things that are technical these days, and the only thing of a technical sort that I can do is communications. The old technical writer was an engineer who got conned into doing some writing and editing. The new technical writer and editor will be a communications expert."

Her present work gives Mrs. V an interest in common with her husband, now manager of a large firm of research scientists working with industry. They dream of working together some day. "He'll have his own company and I'll do all the communications — but that's a long way off."

*Background data*

In Mrs. V's upbringing, the sciences received no particular emphasis. Her father, an accountant, had little or no interest in scientific matters except as they concerned the national econ-

[111]

omy. "But he is very good mechanically. Just for kicks, he's always doing over the house. He's very clever and creative with his hands." His family came from England originally, around the 1600's; the women were always housewives and the men farmers. Later on there were some ministers and lawyers.

Mrs. V describes her father as an old type Yankee — slow, methodical, compulsive. "He was very strict with me. I could go around only with certain people. I was also expected to do lots of things and do them well. And I heard about it when I fell short. My father expected A's, so you had to give him A's. Now that I look back on it, he had the right idea. Because of the training he gave me, I have a very high frustration level — I can take a lot."

Her mother is "the sweet feminine type. She may have done some office work way back, but she married at 18 or 19. My maternal grandmother also was the sweet type. My maternal grandfather came from Denmark. He was a bright guy, very independent — the Germanic type. He was kind of a kook — spoke eleven languages." Mrs. V believes that some of what she calls her rebellious spirit may have come from this grandfather and possibly also from a maternal uncle, an artist. "I thought he was the greatest. He used to send me cartoons he had drawn. So far as I know, one of my brothers is the only one in the family who picked up any of his creative talent. I don't think I really resemble anyone in the family."

The only girl in her immediate family, Mrs. V has twin brothers who are fourteen years older and another brother ten years older. "When I was a youngster, one of the twins was my favorite, but later on I was closest to the youngest brother. He's an accountant. One of the twins is some kind of electronics radio expert; the other is a 'super-duper' salesman. It was like having four fathers. My three brothers, being much older, tried to discipline me just like my father did. They were allowed more freedom and wouldn't let me tag along. This made me kind of

[112]

rebellious, and it also made me want to be a boy in the worst way. I guess I envied the freedom they had."

Growing up in this male atmosphere, Mrs. V developed few feminine interests and pursued mainly masculine activities. "I think that growing up with boys, especially older boys, made me kind of individualistic. I figured boys had so much more fun than girls that I just didn't want to follow the cliché pattern. I guess I got the way I am from rebelling against them rather than from emulating them." She recalled no strong early identifications outside the family.

She does recall, however, identifying vicariously with characters in books, and she read so many that they "merged into one big lump. I ended up being kind of a hodge-podge for a while." When she was in about the second grade, she did identify for a while with one little girl. "She lived in a tiny, doll-type house; never got her clothes dirty and her hair was always curled. She didn't climb trees and wear dungarees or have a dirty face as I did. At the time this seemed so lovely; it was only later that it occurred to me that this girl was a real stupid, fluffy-minded female. I could have a dirty face if I wanted to and still be a girl."

At one time in her childhood, Mrs. V wanted to become a doctor or a nurse, but she was disillusioned when she was hospitalized. With each new life experience, her aspirations changed, but throughout grade and high school, writing persisted as a strong interest. She excelled in English, getting A's on her themes. Although she studied music and dancing, most of her extracurricular activities involved the use of verbal skills. In high school, she was on the debating team and was editor-in chief of the school literary magazine, a job she especially enjoyed because it meant staying late at school.

"As a teenager, I couldn't have been worse. I was uncivilized, a bitch. I was fighting everything and I got pretty fresh on occasion." But she had many outlets for her rebellious feelings —

[113]

writing, dancing, group activities — and she was always encouraged to go on with these activities by *teachers* particularly if she did well in them; this counteracted the rigid discipline at home. Her spirit survived, she learned to conquer some of her aggressive feelings and to overcome frustration.

"I had only a few good friends — I didn't spread myself thin. My standards were high and I moved slowly in making friendships. I was close and loyal to a few and did not play the field.

"The boys were something else again. I had the usual love affairs that ended in hysterics. I would vow never to go out with another boy again, but the next week I was back on the same old merry-go-round. I enjoyed that stuff — I wasn't a recluse with a book. These relationships were very intense while they lasted, but they got to be a bore pretty quickly."

Mrs. V attended a small, provincial and dull high school in a limited size city about forty miles from Boston. The academic standards were poor and she never had to work too hard to get fairly good grades. In her opinion, the teachers were intellectually inferior — "just stuck in their professions." Once in a while, she had teachers who were more challenging. "These are very rare people and they're marvelous. They awaken an interest in you and give you something to go on. I had an English teacher like that." In contrast, she considered her guidance counselor "a stupid, incompetent idiot. She told me I *might* do all right in college. She had absolutely no suggestions about what or where I should study. What I needed at that time was somebody to say to me — go to Radcliffe or Wellesley; you can do it. I would have loved to have gone to one of those challenging colleges, but I used to think I could never, never do it, that you had to have lots of money and an I.Q. of about 160."

Her father decided that "nice girls don't live out of town." So she commuted to a nearby large urban university. "I got a good background there. Anthropology was fascinating and I loved sociology. The study of human relations, by the way, is

[114]

excellent preparation for being a writer — perhaps not in the scientific field, but in creative things — like knocking off a Vance Packard type of job.

"The minute I graduated — bang, wham, off I was. I went to the city, took an apartment with a couple of girls and got a job in a publishing company. It was dull; strictly the secretarial bit. Not for me. You don't get an education just for typing, and taking shorthand, and sitting at a desk being a machine for somebody else's brain." Although she was glad to get a taste of business experience, a year of it was plenty and she was anxious to get started at graduate school in journalism where she earned her degree in three semesters.

There she dated frequently. "But I met very few men who were on my level and still could accept me both as an individual and as a woman. This is rare — men are so damned afraid for their own masculinity. My husband is one of the rare types who wants somebody like me — which makes it very nice. The smarter I am, the better he likes it. He doesn't need to feed his ego on my stupidity — which is the trouble many of my girl friends have with their husbands."

Mrs. V and her husband were married during her final semester at graduate school. They shared many interests and his were as diversified as hers. "He does beautiful abstract work in photography, makes leather holsters, paints a little, and is good with his hands in general. He also collects antiques and has many cultural interests — music, art, and so on." Even as a child he drew models of sport cars and machinery. "He must have read the Encyclopedia Britannica from cover to cover when he was a youngster. His father is a doctor; his mother a registered pharmacist; and an only sister is a laboratory technician as well as an accomplished musician."

Mrs. V attributes her husband's attitude toward women to his mother's influence. "I've got the most fabulous mother-in-law, a strong personality. We get along splendidly. Her family was

[115]

in the drug store business for years. She was very close to her father and enjoyed working with him; he must have been a very understanding guy." Mr. V's uncle, also a pharmacist, still runs the store and Mrs. V's mother-in-law goes there every once in a while to help out, just because she loves it. "I don't know how she became the kind of person she is; Mrs. V's own mother is a very sweet woman, strictly from the feminine school. Yet she was a model back in 1890 or so."

Her family reacted to her marriage and to her job with some concern. "Ours is a mixed marriage from the viewpoint of religion. It had nothing to do with social rebellion. I simply found the only person on earth that I wanted to spend the rest of my life with. At any rate, my family accepts it now.

"As for my job, they probably think I'm peculiar for doing what other people don't do. But they wouldn't tell me what they think about it, although they might tell others, even with a little pride. They go on the principle if you want your kid to do well in something, you don't tell him he's smart; you tell him you expect him to do well. Then, when he succeeds, you say 'that's swell.' You don't overdo it. I had to learn that, too."

Yes, she would bring up her own children this way. "I might not be quite as strict — but not much less. Children should be disciplined. It does them the world of good and helps them discipline themselves. But you can overdo this. I have no patience with strict schedules, for meals and bedtime, for instance. Of course, my husband might not go along with this. He's a bright guy and is completely convinced that any kid we have will be a super-duper genius. I try to tell him he might be just a nice, ordinary kid." Mrs. V believes also that she will be more affectionate with her children than her parents were with her. "And I'll probably do more rewarding than punishing. Also I think a child should learn to appreciate the value of a dollar. Another thing — I intend to surround my kids with educational, intellectual, cultural and artistic things and encourage any talent they

[116]

show. I'll raise my sons as individuals. And I hope they will select wives who are individuals and human beings as well as women — not those fluffy ones."

Mrs. V speaks of having four or five children but *only* if finances permit. "I wouldn't want any of us, including my husband and myself, to be deprived in any way. This may be called selfish, but if I weren't able to go to a symphony or buy an art book when I wanted to, I'd be a bitchy mother. So why have the child? I would prefer mostly boys. I wouldn't know what to do with a girl, really. I'd be afraid she'd turn out like me. I like little boys better, because I don't like women much anyhow. When the boys are in college, maybe in twenty years, my husband and I would be able to do big things together — like having a company of our own. If not, then we would probably go hunting and shooting together. In the meantime, I hope to grow, to mature."

Mrs. V expresses some concern about the broad scope of her interests. "I'm a dilettante when it comes right down to it. My interests are not all laid out. I'm interested in so many things — no set course or goal. One day I may be taking ballet lessons; another, I may be down at the pistol range practicing my target shooting." She readily admits, however, that she likes it this way. "The more hectic, the better; the more things to do in the shortest period of time, the happier I am."

No, she didn't regret the lack of opportunity to go to an outstanding college instead of a large university. "I figure that I gained something from everything that happened. I never regret the past and I never get nostalgic about a past age or a past experience. I like being right where I am — 28 years old in another 20 days, having this husband and this house and these interests. I wouldn't give two cents to be sweet sixteen again."

Although failures upset and depress her, she usually manages to rationalize them on the grounds that they are not her fault. "It's the system. I've had lots of disappointments since graduate

[117]

school — trouble getting a job, for instance. I look younger than I am and not at all like a professional woman. Some people have even refused to interview me just because I'm a female; they'd rather have a man to do the same work if they can get one."

Mrs. V's view of women is firm and uncompromising. She expresses a frank dislike for most women and shows little tolerance, particularly toward those who are "nothing more than sponges who regurgitate their husband's views on everything, or who talk constantly about babies, diapers, and housework, or those who spend an inordinate amount of time and money on their appearance. This is a sore subject. I think a gal's life ought to mean more than the dull existence of a suburban hausfrau. A woman has as much brain as a man and should be entitled to study and advance as far as she can in whatever field she chooses. The Swedes and the Danes have the right idea. After a girl's kids are off to school, she goes out and works; this is looked upon with favor, not with horror. I believe that during a child's formative years mother should be with him, but after he goes to school, why should she live in a vacuum from nine to three?"

Mrs. V believes that society is at fault in all this — that modern woman has lost her identity and has no direction. "Lots of women are trapped; they know they are bored with their lives but don't do anything about it. The average girl, even if she is intelligent, will end up just like the rest of them, doing the things that are expected of her, unless she rebels against the things she doesn't like. As it is now, there are two choices — either you get married or you're a secretary. It takes a lot of guts to get your Ph.D. and it takes more time and work than most women bargain for to become an executive in a high-powered company."

Mrs. V would like to run a salon where stimulating people could gather to discuss world situations, personalities, their own characteristics and concerns, using a tape recorder to pick up certain brilliant statements. In fact, she and another girl have

[118]

already tried it in a small way with a few selected friends. "Much more fun than cocktail parties. The big thing is to get compatible people who think for themselves. Not like so many social gatherings where you scratch the surface and find nothing underneath but a big hole. This is boring."

If she would return to earth after death in any form other than human, Mrs. V would elect to come back as a wild deer. But this seems ridiculous to her. "I'm too egotistical and conceited even to imagine myself as anything but myself." Least, she would want to be a machine or a geological specimen.

*Interpenetration of identity formation and occupational role: psychodynamics of work*

This lively, expressive, creative young woman holds definite, almost intolerant convictions built on a foundation of being different from others and a fighting rebel. This foundation impresses one at first as being solid and secure; in many ways it is. Some of it, however, is a façade. The essence of her identity, which is firmer than that of many her age, centers on that of an independent, fearless, self assured, rebellious intellectual, who hates stereotypes and fetters and has a fighting spirit. It is a pioneer identity like that of her Yankee forebears. But ambivalence abounds. There is a strand of uncertainty; she calls herself a dilettante, needed her high school counselor to tell her to apply to the top colleges rather than taking the initiative herself.

Like the wild deer, free but frightened, that she would like most to be, Mrs. V too has her fearful side. Self-assured, optimistic, even exuberant, proud of her ability as an innovator at work and a rebel against society, she speaks also of often feeling depressed, ugly, and stupid. This does not prevent her from moving forward, taking action and responsibility for **her life**, with the high degree of commitment essential for identity building.

[119]

Most of her enormous rebellion and antipathy are directed at the status of women, the unfairness of society in discriminating against them, and their own shortcomings in being stupid, conforming to the feminine role and wasting their lives as "hausfraus," mothers, wives only. Especially outstanding are her bisexuality and mixed sex identifications. She enjoys shooting (masculine) and ballet (feminine). Hers has been a lifetime struggle against the pull of the feminine current and "trap." She regards herself as more masculine, has a man's way of talking and living, a man's attitudes in general. In fact it seems that her rebellion against femininity is what holds her together, her armor and protection. When it doesn't work, she is depressed. "I get depressed when I cannot fight the system." An active young woman, she needs to be constantly on the go, like the wild deer.

The "sweet, feminine woman," which is the way she describes her mother, is scorned and identification clearly negative. She visualizes her mother as far more beautiful than she, suggesting some difficulty in competing in the triangular situation. It is this, along with the negative identification, which failed Mrs. V in the usual shift towards femininity in mid-adolescence. This failure was reinforced by her ambivalent attitudes for father. He was excessively strict with her, rarely praised her. But he was clever and creative, a "nice guy." Her brothers, too, were overly casual and uninterested; they objected when she wanted to tag along with them, and were favored with special privileges so that she wanted to be a boy too. There seems to have been a paucity of expressed affection or even warmth in the family. Despite her statement that she is unlike any other member, there is actual copying of the men. But this was tempered somewhat by her feeling that they ignored and rejected her, sloughed her off. With her marked need for recognition and response, being ignored was anathema. As she says of herself, "I cannot bear to lose face." She also says: 'Compared with sons, daughters are a catastrophe."

Despite her frank dislike for most women, she admires and is close to her husband's mother who is "good with a screw driver" and mechanically adept — with strong masculine components. Mrs. V can identify with such women, they are like her. Husband's mother may be replacing her own which would be ego-integrating. She also singles out a teacher who awakened her interest in learning. The best way to describe herself, she says with insight: "I am a living example of masculine protest."

It is *her husband* with whom Mrs. V identifies most. He accepts her as both individual and woman which makes her feminine side tolerable. He is both teacher and mentor, as well as brilliant. In such a situation, she relinquishes her rebellion. And he releases her creativity in making the home attractive, and possibly her willingness to have children in whom she does not seem to be highly invested. Babies, she says, are a bore until they show signs of personality development. Husband has facilitated greater ego synthesis.

The handwriting analysis, used because of these limited data derived from a single interview, suggests an active, rather unusual, fantasy life and a self-loving quality. Doing what she wants the way she wants is a must while depression and mood swings are conspicuous. Nor is she always tactful, finds it hard to relax, has little tolerance for the humdrum, run-of-the-mill person, seems to believe only in the elite. Coping mechanisms include activity, rationalization, rigidity and fixed ideas, reaction formation (the restrictions of living at home were intolerable, so she overvalues freedom).

Most of all, she copes through her occupational role. The reciprocity and complementarity between identity and occupation is marked. Besides being masculine and free-lance, the latter gives her the freedom she cherishes; it is prestigious because she is a consultant in a pioneer field so far unsullied by women. It

[121]

involves a technical skill shared by her husband who helps her, and it calls for the writing grace, cognitive gifts and creativity that she possesses. It is an outlet for her creative nature and her curiosity about how things work. The latter perhaps reflecting body curiosity. She shows a high degree of self-acceptance and self awareness.

Her ego development seems to have carried her to the young adult stage where intimacy comprises the crisis. Whether or not the role of mother, especially of girls, will foster personality growth or impose strains is a vital question for the future. Hopefully, the relationship with her husband may help. Mrs. V is a fighter with a massive urge to get what she wants. If she can integrate the two sides of her nature, the masculine and the feminine, more internal unity and harmony may result. So far only a teacher of English served to shape her feminine identity. Her husband, being a role model, serves in a positive way; and her husband's mother even more so because she too is a woman with both masculine and feminine characteristics. Conflicting and vacillating feelings for her father "a nice guy" whose strictness and high expectations for her in contrast with his standards for her more favored brothers who had more freedom all made it hard for her to develop appropriate roles. Yet her behavior and personality are ego-syntonic. She probably derives considerable support from her mother-in-law and the identification between them. Her own mother, "the sweet feminine type," is disposed of cavalierly, but some of the scars from unmet needs for dependency are just below the surface. Mrs. V could not accept her as a female model. Fortunately Mrs. V's capacity for sublimation is high and she is a fighter.

# CHAPTER 8
## Mrs. E: A Young Adult Who Presents a Sharp Contrast to Mrs. V

More like a teenager in appearance than the mother of two, Mrs. E is extremely gracious and restrained, serving coffee and cake when the interviewer arrives. It is hard to convey impressions of her personality; she is not easy to know or talk with. She gives little spontaneous information, often answering questions briefly, occasionally elaborating. Although not an inert individual, she is vague, passive, slightly withdrawn, obviously overdependent and seems to lack stamina. On the other hand she also communicates her sincerity in wanting to help. Her reactivity is minimal.

At a loss for a definite starting subject and prompted by the interviewer, Mrs. E recounted the content of her typical day. She emphasized the point that her main responsibility was to her children — a boy three and a half and one about two. "I get away from the house at least once or twice a week which I find advantageous. Evenings my husband and I enjoy music thoroughly. He is a fine musician and I enjoy listening, but I also play the flute and recorder. And we belong to a Great Books group. I enjoy the neighbors and spend a lot of time drinking coffee with them and watching the children. When I'm free, I go in town and shop; or to a squash game. I was very much of a tomboy as a child, loved football, baseball, and was quite good at them. Playing with dolls wasn't important. I'm still very much interested in sports, like to join in all the activities of the boys. What my toys were before going to school escapes me. *My mother* could tell you a lot better than I."

[123]

*Background data*

The first thing Mrs. E recalls was when she went to the dentist at about two and a half. He told her she shouldn't suck her thumb because her teeth would stick out, and she stopped. Her children do this too, she's sure it's inherited. "I like them to do it; it quiets them down. And I remember that I had a blanket that I put in my mouth, carried around and wouldn't part with. The children do this too.

"I hated school until the fourth grade because I couldn't seem to write without messing things up and got horrible marks. I was the last person in the class to be allowed to use ink. We moved around a bit so that I had to shift schools."

Mrs. E is next to the youngest of four children, with a sister six years older, a brother three years her senior, and a brother three years younger. "My older brother and I were very close, but with the younger one I fought like everything, I guess. High school was fine, I loved it. The teachers I liked best were in mathematics and sciences; these were my best subjects and the teachers stimulated me." Yes, going steady was very much the thing in high school. Mrs. E went steady with one boy for two years.

She doesn't recall *ever* thinking about a career; Mrs. E always wanted to be a mother. Careers were never discussed at home. "Around the seventh grade, we had to fill out some sort of an interest questionnaire about what you want to do after high school, but I never thought much about going to college either. My parents are both college graduates, and so are my older brother and sister but they never brought it up. I used to answer the questionnaire by saying I wanted to be a housewife. Nor did I have any idea of what college I wanted or where, except that going to an all-girl school was out of the question, seemed silly and abnormal. But I finally went to one! Around sophomore or junior year, I decided to go to college — a good one. She selected her "seven sisters" college because one of her mother's friends had gone there; Mrs. E is glad she did.

Her starting major was physics, but she switched to astronomy with a minor in mathematics which was the subject she had excelled in all through school. And she loved and was fascinated with astronomy, although she never entertained the thought of working at it! She got completely wrapped up in it, and adored the professor — a woman. Her strength in the sciences is attributed to a natural ability. "My father is an engineer — an M.I.T. graduate. His two older children had no gift for mathematics so he was very happy when he finally had a daughter who showed an inclination in this direction, and he worked with me sometimes. Father has a lot of traits I admire, honesty and trustworthiness. But he's not the sort you can turn to and talk about your problems. He sometimes likes to pretend that problems don't exist; is even-tempered. His own upbringing was an extremely strict one, and he was that way with the two older children, less so with the younger. My mother is the opposite, shows her feelings, is always analyzing herself and everyone else, see herself as an intellectual which she isn't. She worked for a while in real estate but didn't enjoy it and has always been artistic. Now that she has taken instruction in painting, she does very well. Yes, she analyzes her grandchildren too, but is so wrong. Everything is reduced to a problem when it really isn't and she's always offering suggestions. And works hard at keeping young. [Mrs. E's face flushes when talking of her mother.] But she did intervene by talking with Father when the children wanted something.

"My husband is quite free in expressing feelings and I think it's better that way. He has his doctorate in astrophysics — is way up there in the clouds. Of course he's so far above me that I can hardly bear it. He's a very brilliant, sensitive man. As an undergraduate he minored in astronomy, and he inspired me. He gave a lecture in astronomy, and toward the end of my

[125]

senior year, we were married." Her chief activity in college had consisted of singing in the octet which she led the last year, and in sports competition. She also made some good friends. Usually, she has a best friend, but also mixes with groups.

Her only jobs were for a few months before marriage and six months after. In both, she was a programmer on computers for large companies. "It's probably a terrible thing to say, but I have no interest whatever in returning to work. I like what I'm doing and hope it lasts for a long time. This is contrary to everything we read today. At our reunion, there was a discussion group on the subject of married mothers working. Most of the girls had either returned to work after having children, or had a great deal of conflict about not returning. I don't have any, as a matter of fact I don't have any conflicts."

Mrs. E feels that she is more like her father in temperament and aptitudes. No, it isn't easy for her to express feelings either. Recently she has seen some of mother's traits in herself — traits that she'd just as soon not have. "I kind of wanted a big family, hate to think that two children are all I'll have." Later she says, "I think two is really plenty. Between the children's births I was sick with a glandular disturbance, and they said I shouldn't have any more children. But there was no trouble after the birth of the second child so it's not impossible."

She will probably go along with some of the ways in which she was brought up in rearing her boys except that she won't be as lenient as Mother. "When my father said something, that was it. We're quite strict and feel that limits are important. I expect great things of my boys; they are both brilliant. The younger is musical, could carry a tune at eighteen months. The older boy seems quite mechanical and will probably head toward the scientific field. He's extremely well coordinated. The younger one is very sensitive." This came in response to the interviewer's question about their personalities.

What she would most want to be if she couldn't be human:

[126]

"a fish because I love to swim. It's a nice, easy fun way of living." Least she would want to be a mosquito; "their lives are short and they don't seem to serve much purpose."

Fifteen years from now she would visualize her life as "quite active with what my children do. If they are on the football team, I would go to all the games. Whatever their interests are would include me, especially the Parent Teacher's Association. Financially I should think we'd be reasonably well off."

*Interpenetration of identity formation and occupational role: psychodynamics of work*

Clearly Mrs. E's identity is mother-husband and single track oriented. Apparently she has never thought of a career for herself, even selected a major in college at which she never intended to work. Until the eighth grade when she was assigned an interest questionnaire, she had never thought of different kinds of work. The subjects she liked were the ones identical to father's interests which pleased him. Self-image also included her prowess at sports which has persisted — the perennial tomboy. This is quite characteristic of girls between eight and thirteen but rarer at Mrs. E's age. Although she wanted to attend a boy-girl college, she acquiesced quickly when mother's friend persuaded her to go to a "Seven Sisters" one which she had previously described as silly and abnormal. Mrs. E attended the same camp for ten years, first as a camper, then as a counselor. She emphasized her attachment to the director who influenced her a lot. So did the "adored" astronomy professor, and other teachers. From the above, a mixed sex identity is suggested despite the strong feminine trend. A search for the more perfect mother may also be a dynamic. She is easily influenced by authority figures, appears to be a passive, dependent woman. There is a faint impression of depersonalization. When she could recall no play activities before going to school, she adds in a child-like way: "My mother could tell you."

[127]

Strong and positive identification with her father, husband, and older brother stand out. Whereas father was a martinet with the older children, he relaxed discipline with the younger ones. Mrs. E hints at his preference for her; she shares interests and aptitudes, and like him, she covers her feelings. On the other hand, mother expresses her emotions, was more lenient but the only suggestion of strong negative effect was directed toward mother.

In some ways, husband is a brighter, more highly trained replica of his wife who was up in the clouds too. There may be a tinge of resentment at the gulf between them and at his remoteness. He, too, reveals his feelings. Astronomy may have served as the perfect setting for her fantasy activity which took her away from the routine of her life. Husband gratifies her status and intellectual needs; they have many interests in common. Mrs. E seems to live vicariously through him and through the children. For most prominent is her identification with her sons. Like them she sucked her thumb and carried the treasured blanket. Unlike her mother, she delights in this behavior, and is more permissive in her reactions. But she claims that in general they plan to be strict with the children and set firm limits. She can identify with infantile traits but not with rebellion. She defends with rationalization and undoing, but more outstanding is her use of denial. Like father, she turns her back on troubles, saying "I don't have any conflicts."

Developmentally, there seem to have been some delays at the initiative and autonomy stage as well as that of trust. Her husband has helped her to come to grips with her early relationship with her father but identification with her mother is still quite ambivalent, with marked negative components which have contributed to a confused sex identity. There was sustained rivalry and resentment for her younger brother. Her difficulty in learning to write without messing may be a remnant from the autonomy stage, and her approval of the blanket sucking in the boys,

[128]

suggests reliance on regression — a rather primitive defense. Achievement improved later. She seems to lack firm convictions, conforms to the usual. Nor does she have a strong sense of self. Rather she lives through others, seems unawakened as an individual entity. Her lack of vitality and strange effect may be heightened by her illness, but preceded it by many years. The roles of mother of the boys and wife of a physicist, satisfying to many women, seem overplayed. Now in the intimacy stage, there are suggestions of prolonged adolescence in this child-like mother. Some psychological growth seems to have resulted from marriage and motherhood in her new identifications and what she has learned in caring for the children. I do not feel that I know Mrs. E well enough to have more than a glimpse of her personality and its relation to occupational role.

The way she envisages life fifteen years from now may not win the whole-hearted approval of her then adolescent boys, who developmentally will be seeking independence and liberation from parental ties — at this phase of their lives. Unless she develops as a more special kind of individual with new interests which will serve to moderate her absorption in and high expectations for her sons, participation in their activities may be a devastating disappointment; she may find it hard to release them to emerge as individuals, just when their thrust for independence peaks.

This mother seems to be overidentified with her boys, and plans to relive her life vicariously through them. When the boys grow up and leave home, what will happen to her sense of self? Her husband's expertise makes him a hard person to pace. But she denies conflicts, says she has none! Instead of confronting herself, she restricts her ego and her participation in life.

Yet hers is the kind of life most women choose; it is rarer, however, among college women. Unlike Mrs. V, who is absorbed in her occupation and derives from it considerable gratification, Mrs. E counts on her husband's success and on the

[129]

future achievement of her sons. Her identification with husband and children, earlier with brother, her negative sense of self deriving from mother — all have shaped her life style.

# CHAPTER 9
## Developmental Progress of the Group of Young Adults

The trends drawn from studying this group of young adults — girls five years beyond college graduation — are limited by the relative paucity of our data, which consist of what they told us or omitted to tell us in a single interview. Nor did I have continuous contact with them as I did with Groups I and II subjects when they were in school. What I shall say in the way of interpretation should, therefor, be considered quite provisional.

The age of the subjects ranged from the mid- to the later twenties. I shall report on only eight of the ten cases, four married and four unmarried. All but one of the married group had young children, usually two. Most of these subjects, unlike those in the first two groups, grew up in rural settings. Families again were chiefly of middle-middle social class. Most of them hailed from the mid and far west while the girls in Groups I and II were from the New England area. The parents and grandparents of all but two of the young adults were native Americans. Fathers for the most part held executive status in sizable businesses, or in the academic field. There were also an accountant, a politician, a printer, a combined teacher and farmer, and a production supervisor. Most had finished high school, four were college graduates, one had a doctorate in education, a few had taken specialized technical training. Educational background of the mothers was comparable, with two completing art school on the college level, plus four additional college graduates. Two had been teachers; another started painting as a hobby and is currently successful in selling her work.

It seemed hard for some to speak freely or spontaneously about their parents. Two expressed a strong attachment to and identification with mothers. Another echoed this, but recalled the period of adolescence when they had trouble. Four exploded with vehement negative feelings and identification with either a rigid, forcing and Puritanical mother on the one hand, or one who was too sweet and feminine, on the other. The third was vaguer but resented her mother's intellectual pretensions which were "phoney"; and her interference with and remarks about her grandchildren.

Ambivalent feelings toward the mother which have been so conspicuous in other groups seems to have diminished. These young women are direct and frank. Actually, feelings of love for father are mixed, but positive identification still predominates. A third of the girls spoke of fathers as treating them like the sons they lacked. Three of the group held "only child" status. Identification with brother was not as conspicuous or positive as in the mid-adolescence. One girl referred to him as her "sparring partner"; another as "so unimportant in my life that I was practically an only child."

Along with physical distance from family goes a psychological distance. Identifications have been somewhat vitiated in a number of the girls. A few admire their mother's intellect and competence. Another finds it hard to identify because of mother's hospitalization for an emotional illness. Three are still blatantly hostile, while with another three, the close relationship has been sustained.

The subjects do not differentiate between mother and father as clearly as the younger girls do. They refer to them as parents. With the married group, husbands seem to have upstaged fathers.

Again the subjects in this group emphasized a preference for sports and active boys' games. In two instances where family identity was emphasized to the point of rejection of career, interest in athletics had been sustained so that it was still a major acivity. Almost all were and are great readers (one refers to this as a vice). Some have truly fine minds and like to use them. School has been a source of satisfaction; a few complained about the low level of the teaching in secondary school. "School was one of the few ways in which I could please my parents." Although college was "fun," it was also regarded as somewhat disappointing by a third. One complained that she wanted more contact with the faculty as a source of help in planning her work and her life; another found the student body too conservative and uninterested in politics which she enjoyed. The real blow consisted of having to work exceedingly hard with unsatisfactory results; the feeling of being lost and of lagging behind in a highly competitive group, whereas in high school they had achieved well with a minimum of effort. This experience bruised their confidence and self esteem — the usual freshman "shock." Few of the girls were active extra-curricularly; one sang with a group, a second competed in athletics, a few were house or dormitory managers. One started a chapter of a liberal political organization. "Dating" was, of course, an almost universal activity and preoccupation. "The high point in college was meeting my husband," said two. The girls who married during their junior and senior years improved considerably in their academic work. Perhaps they were able to relax in their concern about social life and competition for men; felt wanted and more secure. Moreover, husband was often busy studying, which released their own time. A cluster of girls tended to lose ground in their course work when dating was going badly; but there was a trend in the reverse direction too: diminished success with men impelled some of the girls to exert greater effort academically.

There were numerous shifts in majors, and uncertainty about occupational goals which were set quite late. Five years later, all had worked for varying periods. Only two of the married subjects were currently working; the lawyer and the mother who was employed part-time; also the technical writer who

[133]

had no children. The balance of the married mothers were at home. One could hardly wait to get back to work or to start graduate school when her children began school. On the other hand the astronomy major, Mrs. E, who was fascinated with and had lost herself in her field, worked as a programmer for a while but harbored no thoughts or conflict about a career since she planned to stay at home, for she was extremely involved with her two "genius-like" boys. Another subject now vacillated between staying at home or working part-time. The unmarried girls worked full time in the professions or semi-professions. All the single subjects had always expected to marry. To one it was her only aim, while the rest thought they might continue working on a part-time basis. One sensed that the married subjects were somewhat more content with their lives; one of the unmarried mentioned her unhappiness five times during the interview. But all was not idyllic in the married group, most of whom felt fenced in and restless, and thought they had lost ground intellectually.

From the handwriting analysis, earliest memories, Pigem Test, and bits of what the girls say, we glean a little more about their images of selves, and their less overt feelings. One girl who was affable and compliant in the interview became derisive and avoidant when finishing sentences on the Sentence Completion Test. Disguised aggression was clear in her handwriting. So, too, was there a lack of trustworthiness in an over-moralistic subject. Quite a cluster of girls displayed in handwriting covert masculine tendencies stronger than usual. Half of the girls showed an inclination toward science, and this may stem from the strength of identification with fathers. Three girls refer to themselves as lazy, tending to drift, as weak characters — yet also conscientious; two as opinionated, egotistical, dogmatic and overly frank. Almost half feared being "kicked out" if they displayed their rages at home. Mothers are reported to be very ambitious for their daughters while fathers

[134]

are proud of them and have "quieter aspirations." Confidence goes in the direction of use of the intellect rather than toward interpersonal relations. About a third speak of being socially backwards, not sought after. Half of the married group plan to limit their families and have no more children.

Singular in this group is the new, cogent, and compelling influence of the husband. The subjects tell about them with pride and spontaneity for the most part. Actually they have married men who are high achievers in the upper level professions. Three of the eight hold doctorates in medicine, astrophysics, and crystallography. The achievement of the men seems to moderate the status strivings of their wives for professional prominence. They become practical in planning for part-time work which can be fitted into their busy schedules. All but one of the men support their wives' desire to work outside the home when the children are in school; view them as having more than one possible life. One man feels that social work should be a good field for his spouse, and she is investigating.

The lawyer caught her husband's enthusiasm for law and they went through law school together. This bolstering of the wife's career interests as well as other facets of her life has a firming effect on her identity. But an interesting finding is that the seed of the interest dates back to identification with father. Our lawyer's father, who was in politics as she is in a small way, wanted to study law himself; encouraged daughter's inclination, took her to senate hearings. Husbands and fathers were described in almost identical terms. One girl said she was living out her father's dream by becoming the first college graduate in the family. Through the new identification with husband, some of the girls seem to have come to terms with the oedipal situation and/or the latter may have been instrumental in the choice of spouse. Outside of this group we know other wives who have switched to their husbands' profession, notably a biochemist who earned a doctorate in clinical psychology after marrying a psychiatrist.

Developmentally, we can speak, again tentatively, of the identity and intimacy stages of the young adults. The latter is called the period of post-adolescence by Blos and viewed as a transition from childhood to adolescence which can be analyzed from either angle. In the majority of subjects, identity seems to have stiffened. They have firmer convictions, take quite definite stands, are less dependent on what people say, show greater independence, have settled on an occupational choice. Values have crystallized and important syntheses have been partly achieved. Continuity and self-sameness have been matched by the meaning which goes with their acceptance and recognition by the community.

In this life-period, the task is to come to terms with parents' ego interests. Competition and antagonism for mother recedes and most of the young adults make peace with their mothers' image. Blos (1962) cites the instance of the young mother who had formerly opposed order and resisted identification with the "good" mother, but now takes pride in being a good housekeeper which she acknowledges learning from mother. The implementation of goals in terms of permanent relationships, roles, milieu choices becomes of foremost concern, and the individual elaborates her special way of life, decides between such polarities as material gain versus the scholarly life. Important, too, in this period is the achievement of balance between harmonizing instinctual strivings and ego values. "The psychosexual task of the girl is normally brought to completion through motherhood and post-adolescence has achieved its special gain when the personality can permit parenthood to make its specific contribution to personality growth. . ." For those who do not marry, sublimation in work and friendship make their particular gift.

One roadblock to psychic maturity at this period, says Blos, is the rescue fantasy, the wish to be rescued by circumstances

[136]

in the form of an individual or luck. "If I only had another job or were married or prettier," they think, "life would be better."

Erikson (1963) refers to this period as the intimacy stage and its opposite isolation — also as the period of moratorium when the individual through role experimentation may find a niche in some section of society, a niche firmly defined, yet which seems uniquely made for him. In finding it the young adults gain an assured inner continuity and social sameness which will bridge what she was as a child, what she is about to become, and will reconcile her conception of herself and her community's recognition of her. "The young adult is eager and willing to fuse his [or her] identity with that of others. Body and ego must now be masters of the organ modes and nuclear conflicts (sufficiently) to face the fear of ego loss in situations which call for self abandon, in the solidarity of close affiliations and friendships, in orgasms and sexual unions, in experiences of inspiration by teachers and of institutions from the recesses of self."

No attempt was made to elicit information on the sexual life of our subjects in a single interview; attention will therefore focus on ego values. Some of the subjects may be stating this understanding, if not acceptance, in a rather indirect and subtle way. For the first time, half of the subjects in this group raise a new topic; they acknowledge somewhat ruefully that they are now aware of characteristics in themselves similar to those disliked in their mothers. Like mother the subject gets upset easily, or is a worrier, or moody or needs constant activity. Is this a reflection of delayed internalization of qualities formerly rejected, now accepted by the more tolerant daughters who are reacting to realistic pressures, or have they unconsciously imitated mothers in a primitive way, as the baby bird does in learning to fly. Or is there a factor of genetic similarity at work?

The rescue fantasy is quite clear in a number of the girls,

[137]

especially as it relates to marriage and a better job. The former is, of course, especially important in the lives of the single subjects. Although quite uneasy in their friendships earlier, now they have found more comfortable relationships with both sexes; some have achieved a sense of belonging, of sublimation. Earning a living and managing money enhances their independence and practical sense. About a third of the group mention teachers who have been inspiring, about the same proportion have considerable insight into themselves. The criterion of psychological growth through motherhood or through sublimated work and growth affiliations is met by approximately half the group. Where the relationship was consistently negative and the mother rigid and unaccepting in her role, some slight improvement may take place but the identification remains essentially negative. Sometimes rather serious discordance between instinctual expression and ego values persists.

The older girls express fewer altruistic attitudes about jobs as compared with the younger ones. There is less identification with family members, siblings, aunts, grandparents. The young adults indulge in fantasy far less than the younger girls, are quite reality-oriented, even find it hard to respond to projective questions or to recover early memories. The two exceptions were highly fanciful girls who had no siblings.

Only one girl in the group is bored with her work, and this has happened to her on other jobs. She tends to be overcritical and negative; her goal is marriage. For the most part, the choices these girls have made feature a reciprocal push-pull relationship between identity formation and occupational role. This lends unity to their ego and substance to the scaffolding of their identities as well as to their role performances. Added to this is the evolving of identity deriving from husbands if the marriages are so-called "good" ones, featuring mutuality. We cannot evaluate or predict this, but these couples seem to share

[138]

many interests. The marriages however are still fresh and untouched by blight.

About half see their parents' marriages as unhappy, and hope to be better wives and mothers. They are still planning their lives, and seem absorbed with the dilemma of how to combine part-time work or school with their homemaking role. For these are mostly girls who like to use their minds. Some anxiety as to whether or not this can be accomplished without harming the children psychologically pervades their outlook. But they also want to remain interesting persons, especially in the eyes of their husbands, rather than "falling asleep after dinner as I do when I'm home with the children all day." With a few exceptions, they try to give the impression of psychological well-being, and underplay the concerns that really bother them. Two, however, acknowledged spontaneously that they may have "asked for" some of the early troubles at home. Intimacy, it is clear, revolves around maturity in a complex way.

Two young adults mentioned when they returned to work part-time, that they had the best of two possible worlds.

The integrative, calm period of late adolescence succeeds the turmoil of mid-adolescence, while the new quality of the love readies the young adults for intimacy and avoids the other polarity called isolation. Subjects are strongly invested in marriage and motherhood.

The vitally significant choice of a husband takes place and the subject is aided by a more completely formed identity, for she fits her new identification with husband into what she has assimilated and made her own. Important, too, is the "home of one's own," which lends distance from parents, the father in particular. The husband plays the role of loosening the grip of oedipal attachments. Distance from the family is also psychological in nature. But the young woman becomes interested in parents' ego attitudes, enjoys visiting them. The relationship with the mother is less competitive and more comfortable for more than half of the women. Children give them the opportunity for additional psychological growth. About half of the young adults are unmarried in the late 1960's. Friends of both sexes and attitudes toward their occupations assume significance; yet these subjects volunteer the information that they would prefer to be married. They are in the establishment period of occupational development and are trying to make a place for themselves in it.

# CHAPTER 10
## Miss S: A Classic Career Woman in the Generative Stage

A personable woman in her early forties, Miss S expresses herself in satirical and humorously self-disparaging superlatives. Originally, she had limited the talk with the interviewer to one hour, later offering additional information should it be needed, and also asking her secretary not to interrupt us.

Miss S holds the highly responsible job of chief stylist in a large chain of shops with many branches. "We've become gatherers, communicators, and a clearing house of information on fashion which is ever-changing. Because we have an overview of all segments of the fashion world, we organize the trends for the benefit of the people who buy and sell the merchandise. We help the former to select from the many trends available. Then we work closely with the advertising and display departments, as well as with publicity; are responsible for the style shows, talk with the training department. Overall, we try to help make this store stand for the newest, most exciting and appealing fashions in town.

"The fascinating thing which also could be termed the curse of the field is the relation of fashion to what is going on in the world. One can never get away from it: at the theatre you find yourself constantly observing; on a beach at a Caribbean island, the eye roams over the type of bathing suit worn. Getting along well with all sorts of people, and coordinating functions make up another important part of the job."

*Background data*
How did she progress to such a job? Miss S thought the inter-

[141]

viewer would not learn much from what catapulted her into it because the whole thing was freakish, an accident; it was hard to sketch a route to it. "It all goes back to the summer after I was graduated from high school in the mid-west. I was a very fat youngster and all my friends were going to be models in a fashion show for girls entering college. Not being the model type, and not wanting to be left out, I went to the advertising manager of the large department store and told her that all her problems were solved because I would write and produce the show. She was desperate enough to let me do it and later the president of the store said I could come back any time I wanted. So I had a wonderful year at college and on returning from a fun-summer vacation, found a message to call him. He offered me a job for the summer in the advertising department. I developed an idea for a radio program and it had enough merit for them to be willing to try it, but only on a thirteen-week basis. So I had to decide whether to stay or return to college and I decided to stay, much to the disappointment of my parents. It worked out happily enough. This job was what I wanted; I could always return to college. And then I had an extremely good break — the advertising manager retired and at age nineteen I was given her job."

Miss S's next job came about through a "freak" too. She had been doing a promotion with a large organization in the east, and it ran into snags which brought a company executive out to see her. They "hit it off well," and he offered her a job with his company in sales promotion. She was quite satisfied with her present job, and made all sorts of demands which he met. She knew she would go east at some time, so finally accepted and at age 20 came to this vicinity. After a year, she left because she knew her destiny lay in the retail field, and thought some manufacturing experience would round out her qualifications. After a stint at that, she wanted to try her hand at her own business as consultant in retail fashion production.

[142]

Next came an attractive offer from her present employers to start in as copy writer in the advertising department. She has been there now for over ten years, rising to her current role about five years ago.

In every career, there is a key person; Miss S thought in hers it was the president of the store who gave her her first job. "I think it was absolutely extraordinary that he had enough confidence in an ignorant, green youngster to give her a job of considerable authority in which the budget was a large one; that he believed in me enough. If retailing runs in your blood, you're not happy in anything else although it's demanding and tiring. Yet if anyone had asked me about my professional plans as a child, it would have been farthest from my mind."

Even at age nine or ten, she had talked of becoming a journalist and of writing the great American novel. Later when she got interested in theater, she thought of turning it into a play; and in college she planned to major in journalism. Editing the school magazine was her chief activity in high school. Yes, she did writing in her copy job, and now does a long, overall summary of each season's fashion trends. Writing is a major part of her work. She is a "Sunday painter," interested in and with some talent for color, line, design, and texture, but rather poor at drawing which could have been a help in sketching clothes.

Frequently Miss S referred to herself as a very ordinary sort of person, prosaic, run of the mill, but happy. "I was the world's number one tomboy, couldn't have been less interested in clothes or in dolls. Bikes or baseball bats fascinated me; and on rainy days, I sat at my desk fancying I was the editor of the New York Times. It was the writing and producing of the style show and being with my friends that motivated me. Obviously taste and the other skills can be developed; you are not born with them." As early memories, the things that come to mind have to do with being in trouble, such as "throwing a light bulb against the wall in a fit of temper, getting glass in my eye; and

[143]

swallowing a fly swatter, the handle only. I hadn't responded to being called for dinner and fell when the maid chased me. I guess I was a little monster. And I always cadged food since I was so fat that my mother regulated my diet."

An only child, Miss S attaches little importance to this. "I had lots of friends, was outgoing and gregarious. I still take friendships very seriously. My relationships with my parents were very happy; they are intelligent and this may be why I didn't mind being the only one." The high intelligence of her parents was stressed; father was somewhat brighter than mother, who was the dominant parent, however. "They were quite permissive, believed I would be happiest doing what I wanted, although they wouldn't let me do improper things. Her grandfather gave her an expensive typewriter for her tenth birthday and was pleased with the journalism ambition. She has qualities of both parents. "My mother and I have identical tastes. She was always very interested in clothes and fashions, has always been a well-dressed, very attractive woman. But this didn't foster my interests because I was always the fat child, as well as the fat adult until my recent illness. In disposition, I'm more like my father. Both of us are essentially salesmen." Before his present business, father had operated a retail store.

Parents expressed no objection to her leaving home for the job in the east. "If they had said, 'we're going to miss you' or 'it will be lonesome in the house,' I would have stayed."

Miss S feels that she's well adjusted, and by nature a happy person, very normal and functioning within a normal framework. Were she to have a second chance for choice of career, it would be something related to writing and the theater. "But I would not have made as good a living as I do. And I'm nomadic by instinct, enjoy travelling, and would like to be able to pick up and go whenever the spirit moved me."

How did she see her life ten years from now? Miss S was generally too busy thinking about today. "I can't imagine myself not being professionally involved, and if I have a formal career, this shop is the place I would like it to be. There is no other higher job that I have my eye on. As values, people will always be important to me and certainly my work. I can't visualize a life without either. Of course, I would like to get married, but could never dream of marrying a man who would object to my career. Comfortable standards of living are important to me, money for attractive living, for theater, symphony, travel. Since I have been ill, I value health a good deal." Her job calls for considerable travel — both to other Eastern cities and to Europe.

With the exception of mothers with very young children, she feels that work makes women more stimulating; helps them become more of a person. Whether or not a husband is understanding makes a vast difference. Miss S feels that destiny plays a large part in one's life; but that one must "ride with the tides. And we wind up where we never thought we would."

*Interpenetration of identity formation and occupational role: psychodynamics of work*

Despite Miss S's insistence that she was catapulted into her job which was freakish and an out-of-pattern accident; she is a strong believer in destiny, and speaks of her current work in the retail field as being "in my blood." Yet she also regards the man who gave her her first job as the "key" person in her career because he had enough confidence in an untried child to give her a responsible job identification. With this last as an exception, she seems to be aware of only surface motivation for her choice of occupational role. But she does not appear to see herself as the agent who initiated and sold ideas or the job as requiring superior cognitive skill and versatility; or that it affords the opportunity to use her writing skill and aspirations in reporting the trends of the times in their relation to style, and formerly in the creation of advertising copy. Moreover, the

[145]

setting appeals to her outgoing, active life style, gives her the opportunity to travel, status, and a sizable income which provides the comforts she cherishes.

There may be some less conscious reciprocity between her self image as ugly, fat, ordinary and clown-like and the gratification inherent in her task of glamorizing other women — a sublimation. Her mother, whom she describes as attractive, slender, and interested in clothes — probably plays an important part here as a positive identification figure but as also one with whom she competes; the negative aspect may derive partially from mother's depriving Miss S of the food she liked and more in her inability to empathize with her daughter's feelings about the deprivation and the obesity itself. Mother's attractiveness, in contrast to what daughter perceived as serious physical deviations in her appearance may, too, have complicated resolution of the oedipal situation. With father, identifications seem more positive; she is like him in temperament and in the nature of his early work as retailer. There are also identifications with the man who gave her the first job, who trusted her, and with grandfather who showed confidence in her journalistic aspirations by giving her a typewriter. It is the male rather than the mother who is the "giving" person — a reversal of roles. And she identifies especially with her peers.

It is not easy to know and understand the identity of Miss S, who seems to have taken on the protective coloration of her field. Her recounting of her early life experiences is undifferentiated and incomplete; and it is all a bit too consistently perfect. She seems to have been a child from whom a good deal was expected, one who was taught to keep things to herself, to conceal her feelings in spartan fashion, and to conform. Around the time Miss S was wrestling with the decision about coming east, she had broken her engagement to a man whom she regarded as not ambitious enough. We can only wonder whether this factor was instrumental in her parents' willingness for her

[146]

to settle so far from home. The tone of the subject's statement that she would have stayed had her parents spoken of missing her has a wistful, nostalgic ring of dependency and desire to be wanted, although independence seems to be the hallmark of her life.

Far from being an "ordinary, prosaic, run-of-the-mill" individual, Miss S is a highly intelligent, competent, imaginative woman with a wide range of abilities, talent and achievement drive. But her life has not been as perfect as she suggests. That she has had her times of trouble is suggested by her angry, violent early memories of throwing a glass. Her handwriting suggests the adoption of a stylized façade, and concern with the "thing to do," with what people think of her, with money and possessions. There seems to be more-than-average depression, which may be a factor emanating from her recent surgery. Coping mechanisms feature flexibility, the ability to detour around difficulties, and to sublimate her work in travel, and in outside interests, particularly her creative activity as a "Sunday painter" who has sold some of her work.

Her history illustrates what the occupational role can do for identity formation in reinforcing self-esteem, confidence, and in finding a place where she feels she belongs. In beautifying others, perhaps she is partaking of the beauty herself, repeating and delaying a worry of long standing. Her need for a façade, however, suggests some weak spots in her self-awareness and sense of self; and she wears the uniform of her career well, and plays roles. But her occupational and group identities are both strong and supporting. What also stands out is her *adaptive strength* in her first job when she substituted the writing and production of the style show — a task in which she excelled, for the modeling work of her friends from which she was ruled out.

Miss S is now in the generative stage of her life. As Erikson has defined it, "this is primarily the concern in establishing

[147]

and guiding the next generation. Some do not apply this drive to their offspring — and indeed the concept is meant to include more popular synonyms as 'productivity and creativity' which, however, cannot replace it." Both productivity and creativity rank high in her job performance. She seems to regard career success with its concomitant financial advantages above that of marriage and children; the direction of her identity is single track and career oriented. It is possible that she is performing the task of generativity in her training of and relationships with young workers.

Techniques include frequent identifications, positive with father, less so with mother. Characteristics were prominent earlier than usual, as are sublimation of the masculine side stressed in her tomboy experiences. Fragments of the repetition-compulsion are also visible in activating her life.

## CHAPTER 11
### Mrs. N: A Retread Nurse

A fresh-looking woman in her late forties, Mrs. N stands out from other subjects in her enthusiasm and interest in participating in the talk, repeating that it was enjoyable and useful. It was a new role for her to be doing most of the talking, and she thought most other subjects had probably had more interesting lives. "While I've been talking, I've also been thinking . . ." Mrs. N is the mother of four who will have to be making decisions about career, and has always been curious about how and where these begin. Her husband is an engineer.

Mrs. N recounted the evolving of her own profession of choice — nursing, of being ill with a contagious disease when she was ten. She was cared for by a nurse who was the only person allowed in the room. "Because of our isolation from the rest of the family, we had sort of a concentrated time to talk. It was just conversation but I asked a lot of questions on how you do this and that and why. But I do know that from that experience on I went around saying 'I'm going to be a nurse'. It's curious — I remember her name and that she was not especially prepossessing . . . not a nanny type in the sense of motherliness. All I remember is that she was fun and I liked to have her there, didn't resent being quarantined and felt comfortable with her.

"Even as a small child, I was always more interested in people than in things. At the same time I was quite shy. The family would say, 'Here we're all going sailing and E is staying home to say goodbye to someone who was leaving after vacation.' Even in playing with my doll, I never pretended it was

[149]

my own; it was someone to take care of. I'd get out my mother's Dr. Holt [the Dr. Spock of that era] and find out how to do it.

"I'm the oldest in the family with two brothers (we're all about eighteen months apart) and I'm afraid I was pretty much the bossy oldest. This wasn't all to my advantage: it was 'you should know better or you can do it because you're older.' We played together a lot and I tried to compete in their rough-house games. One of my brothers is an experimental psychologist and a university professor. The neighborhood had far more boys than girls, but I had two very close girl friends. In high school there was also a "crowd." We talked endlessly, walked, and played bridge. My parents had their hearts set on a particular Seven Sisters' college for me, and never admitted that I might do anything else; they accepted the nursing ambition but wanted to make sure I had a good college education first. That summer I heard of a course combining both, and rushed to tell them that I had found a way to have both the degree they wanted and the nursing I wanted. But I had to do a lot of justifying because my parents were used to thinking of college as a liberal arts education. And I was thrilled that I would be starting in with the things that interested me — those relating to nursing."

There was little "going steady" while Mrs. N was growing up, but she has strong feelings against it, and has worked in the community to diminish the custom. Organization-wise, Mrs. N leads a busy life, is on the board of directors of a number of social agencies, active in the P.T.A., enjoys this kind of life more than the chores of housework. Now that she has committed herself to volunteering as a nurse at a hospital a day a week, she has had to reduce her schedule. This, she believes, is a step toward returning to the field; she is also considering a retraining course for nurses. Her husband, an engineer, has reacted positively but says "no more P.T.A. I've had it."

"In high school I tutored a younger girl in geometry and liked it. I asked my father: 'Do you think I ought to be a

[150]

teacher?' He said, 'Maybe but think about whether you want to go over the same material every year.' " Mrs. N thinks she is more like her father than mother. "It's harder to explain things to her; she doesn't express much interest and is reserved in her praise, whereas he voiced it profusely. There were also three quite fascinating grandparents whom I adored. Decisions were usually talked over at dinnertable; we spent a long time eating." Any decision or criticism involving time limits on getting home from dates awaited the absence of her two brothers; her parents did not discuss her rule-breaking in front of others. Mostly they decided things but in a non-authoritative way. "On some subjects I couldn't move them. I would get quite excited about things but don't recall much ill feeling. From 14 to 17 was a hard time. All my experiences were heightened. Everything was either very thrilling and inspiring or very tragic and depressing. But this was here today and gone tomorrow.

"My father trained as a chemist and was an executive in a mill. I think he was disappointed with business and might have preferred pure chemistry. He was a great reader and liked the scholarly life. My father was probably the dominant one; my mother leaned on him, felt he was the 'man of the house,' and that it should revolve around him. She would say: 'Daddy will be home and we will have supper at such a time, and we will give him the piece of chicken he likes.' They presented a united front on most things. Yes, my children have been brought up in the same way except I have tried to include them in more discussions around planning. Eating everything on their plates wasn't as important to us as to our parents.

"One of my earliest memories at around five was of trying to prepare coffee with an alcohol lamp and setting fire to the house. I yelled for my parents who extinguished it, and in general were quite calm and not angry with me." She remembers with pleasure growing up in Northern New England, enjoying the beauty, the freedom of outdoor life and unlimited space

[151]

"even though I had been told by a neighbor that the woods were full of bears." This was when Mrs. N was around 3; she can still see the trillium blooming.

"I went to a very small private school with about five in the class. We all knew each other well and had plenty of attention from the teacher. There were two special highlights: one, we stood around the piano and sang; and there was a crippled teacher whom I liked very much. I always got to school early, never had strong feelings about 'that horrible math.' Yet I was happy when vacation came. I read quite a lot but wasn't a bookworm. *Green Mansions* was one of my favorites. During my nurse's training I didn't read at all. Everything I started seemed so bland and watered down compared with the slice of real life I was seeing. My family all read a great deal. My mother was never active in the community."

To jump ahead, both high school and college were fun, particularly the latter. After graduation she worked mostly in public health and went to the patients' homes. The doctor left concise orders, but the nurse had the responsibility for deciding when to call him, and members of the family depended on her. "I worked in one district which had a warm, friendly supervisor for about eight months. My supervisor thought I had a tendency to go ahead too fast, and I did. Quite soon I was made assistant supervisor, but the new job didn't work out too well. The supervisor was out ill, and there was no one to brief me. So I was transferred back to staff nurse status, but I had no sense of demotion for I knew I wasn't ready to supervise and enjoyed the direct work with the patient at home and as part of a family.

"After a year, I decided to marry, but worked until the seventh month of pregnancy. All this time I was sharing an apartment with two other girls and it was a lively, pleasurable time of life. At college, I had the chance of taking the Head nurses' Administration Specialty, but turned it down. Some of

[152]

the students had trouble with the operating room training. It never bothered me because I thought in terms of this as something we can fix. Actually it's quite neat and orderly; you can see only part of the patient, and there's a definite routine with everybody working together. The patient acutely ill in his bed is more awesome. You see the whole person and you know it's touch and go, and a lot has to be done for him quickly, so let's do it.

"When my oldest child was a little over two, and the other an infant, my husband went into the service and was overseas for about five years. This was the time when there was a desperate need for nurses in general and specifically for the victims of the Cocoanut Grove fire. I settled the problem by working nights, and getting home in the morning after the children's naps. It seemed important not to have the babies feel that both parents had left. And I'd go to sleep with the children until the sitter came, yet didn't get much sleep. But I kept it up for two years and then did occasional 'specialing' for friends.

"My husband is less gregarious and more of a scholar than I. Now that we have two more children he decided that he would transfer from teaching to consulting work, and has also written textbooks to earn more. What I would really like is to work with him; were he a doctor I could." Both he and the children ask her about her experiences at the hospital. "Eventually I will need a refresher course. My uncle, an eighty-year-old practicing pediatrician, disagrees, and believes that bedside care is the important factor." Yes, she always admired him but never thought of becoming a doctor; the field is too complex. "Were I to have a second chance, I would keep up my professional knowledge and skills."

Mrs. N spoke perceptively about her children, individualizing each. As parents, they would like to see the children through college and graduate school, happily married and leading good

[153]

lives. It would be disappointing to both parents if the children didn't continue their education beyond high school.

About eighteen months after our talk, we learned that Mrs. N had enrolled in a retraining course for nurses, after which she took a full-time, quite arduous job with the public health department, traveling from town to town throughout the state. Despite illness and additional responsibility for her failing mother, she has continued her work. A sad period marked the death of her father a few years ago.

*Interpenetration of identity formation and occupational role: psychodynamics of work*

Mrs. N seems to be a warm, outgoing, open woman, positive, practical and high principled in her attitudes, yet accepting of others. A clearly altruistic pattern runs through her life. Yet she views herself as rather run-of-the-mill, not outstanding in any way, very shy. Hers is a good life in terms of a happy childhood, and successful school and college experiences. Rather simple and unassuming, Mrs. N tends to denigrate herself; gives the impression that she may repress intense feelings or drives, especially in expressing hostility. Her stance is more that of the Golden Mean. She keeps the talk on an overt rather than covert level. Disappointments are absorbed; she expends great effort on things that are important to her, such as arranging for nurses' training on a college level.

Her lack of success at the assistant supervisor's job did not seem to upset her, nor did she resent the demotion. What she wants to do and do well is quite clear to her; she has a high degree of self-awareness and a special sympathy for people who are ill. Quite striking is her positive response to community needs, as illustrated by her return to nursing during the war. This called for real personal sacrifice and hardship — the apex of fidelity in the identity structure. Rather than brooding over her husband's long absence, she performed the jobs of three

[154]

people — mother, father, and nurse. Surface feelings seem quite available to her; so are the feelings of others.

Her parents appear to be kind, calm, realistic individuals who did not over-envelop her with love, but had high educational aspirations and perceived her as an individual. She had a special rapport with father; they really communicated and he encouraged her. She admired his scholarliness and open-mindedness. With mother, identification is more ambivalent; it is hard for a child to have an unresponsive mother. There must also have been positive identifications judging from the feminine orientation in Mrs. N's personality. The quality of mothering evident in her work and with her own children seems warm, reflective, and sensitive. Perhaps she is sparked by a wish to do better than her mother, to differentiate herself. Her two older children are currently successful in graduate school, both candidates for the doctorate. What she would do were they to reject higher education, we do not know. The youngest child plans to be a nurse.

The powerful identification with the nurse who cared for her when she was isolated with a contagious illness undoubtedly affected Mrs. N's choice. Her nurse's very presence made Mrs. N feel secure and comfortable. For the crippled teacher, too, she seemed to have special feeling almost by virtue of the defect. Compassion for the ill or handicapped stand out.

Identity has been forged adaptively. Mrs. N knew what she wanted from an early age, and had sufficient belief in herself to pursue and fight for it. While her children were growing up, she served indirectly through volunteering for social agencies. She has a genuine identity, germane to her whole value system and convictions. Although she and her husband are quite different in temperament, they seem to have made a fairly good life together insofar as we know.

Identity formation and occupational role flow and blend into each other, nourishing both. This reciprocity heightens con-

[155]

tinuity as well as a good degree of integration and synthesis. The tasks of the stages of intimacy and generativity appear to have been met successfully. Since she thinks of herself as a particularly shy person, nursing allows for a special kind of intimacy within a structured, egosyncratic situation.

## CHAPTER 12
### Developmental Progress of Groups in Generative and Integrative Stages

About 90 per cent of the ten mature women are in the generative versus stagnation stage; one is in the age of integrity. The former is the stage concerned with establishing and guiding the next generation, one's own children, those of relatives, or children who are supervised by organizations. Erikson includes the qualities of productivity and creativity in his presentation of this phase. There is a libidinal investment in what is being generated; the ability to love oneself in the meeting of the minds. Just having children or wanting children does not constitute generativity; some young people experience difficulty in the realization of this wish, trouble reaching back to early childhood impressions, excessive self-love, some lack of faith, only slight belief in the species.

It would seem that some professions by virtue of their nature fit the criteria: nursing, teaching, social work, all have opportunities for generative life. A number would qualify on the creativity and productive criteria.

Most women are striving to hold their place. The wide age range in this group of mature women may attenuate the clear-cut nature of the clusters and regularities. A few of the subjects are in their late forties, some in the fifties and one in the sixties. The modal age falls at the early fifties. The group spans two stages: generativity and integrity, with only one in the latter. There is, however, sufficient variety to influence their outlook on lives.

As in the Young Adults, information is based on a single interview. Interpretations are, therefore, offered as exploratory and

[157]

tentative. Although I am reporting on only a few subjects, calculations of percentages are based on all ten in the group. Five of the women are married and have children, one is now divorced and the balance unmarried. Middle-middle class families again predominate. A few of them hail from the south or midwest; most are from nearby areas. All but one are native born, as are their parents and grandparents in most instances.

Self-built businesses which had become medium size companies seemed prevalent. But there were also a number of professional fathers. Another father had died before his daughter was born. About a third of the men had continued their education. Education of the mothers lagged behind that of their husbands, reflecting perhaps the cultural situation of times when it was unusual for women to attend college. Yet all but four mothers had continued and completed college, one had her doctorate, two had done graduate work and one was engaged in it.

The unmarried subjects worked full-time as teachers, writers, fashion expert; the married as nurse, a top level psychologist, graduate student, and a school guidance counselor. Despite the advent of children, there have been only a few interruptions; and these were quite short. This raises an interesting point: despite the hardship of combining child care and outside occupations, some of the highly trained are motivated to make this effort. Two of the writers worked intermittently. One subject had retired after a long career as a teacher.

Almost all have been quite close to and identified with fathers. One described this parent as a "source of inspiration." Father is considered more intelligent and sympathetic than mothers. The woman whose father died before her birth has a remarkably close and positive relationship with her mother who is a fine role model and tries to play the part of both parents. With the exception of one subject who is quite disturbed and claims to flagrantly hate her mother, relationships are now far more

[158]

peaceful and less intense, however, than in the growing-up period. This supports the thesis that developmentally, daughters express more affection and are increasingly identified with mothers after adolescent fantasies have waned. But only two subjects mentioned having happy homes.

There are strikingly similar patterns between fathers and the men the subjects married. In this group as well as its predecessor, a subject whose father was an insurance executive married a man in the same field. This happened, too, in two other families. Half of the women spoke of the similarity in temperament of father and husband.

All of the unmarried wanted ultimately to marry. One qualified her statement, adding that this held on condition that she didn't have to reduce her luxurious standard of living. In the instance of a professional wife, she and her older husband have reversed roles somewhat, so that he takes considerable responsibility for the children and for purchasing the food while she in turn refuses to attend evening professional meetings so that she can spend the time at home.

In this group there is also an example of a clear-cut identification with a nurse who cared for the subject when she was ill as a child with a contagious disease. Subject, too, became a nurse and in other ways modeled her life on her ego ideal. Heroes from books also appeared to sway these mature women. Brothers and sisters are mentioned infrequently; most live in distant communities. But at the peak of the competitive years, rivalry seemed milder perhaps partially because brothers were much younger.

One bit of dramatic regularity appears in the responses to the Pigem Test. "If they could return to the world after death but could not be human, with but one exception, *all would most like to* be birds. This pattern also appeared in the pre-adolescents. Their elaboration of the wish suggests that it may represent a wish for freedom, but not the kind of freedom sought by

[159]

the pre-adolescents. Here the bird may represent a recapturing of youth with its easy, quick movements and its absence of body restriction and restoration of personal beauty. The bird is often described as a pretty one. Apprehension about aging and fear of death are mentioned by more than a third of the women. Some have turned for comfort to study of religions that feature reincarnation. This may be in part a resurgence of death fears expressed in more disguised form in the mid- and, to a slightly lesser degree, in the pre-adolescents. Subjects in these groups are also trying to deal with the instinctual thrust by defending through the spiritual and by activity.

Erikson (1963) in his section on ego integrity versus disgust or despair in old age, writes: "The lack or loss of this accrued ego integration (the acceptance of one's one and only life cycle as one which had to be) is signified by a haunting fear of death; the one and only life cycle is not accepted as the ultimate of life." Deutch (1945) mentions this as quite similar to the situation of women in the pre- and early climacterium. And both maturation and mid-adolescence are crisis periods which mark turning points in life. Some of the mature women are realistically encountering beginning old age or poor health and want to show what they can do with their lives as a last or second fling — to enrich and make useful and productive the years left. Some remarked on their happiness in returning to work. "I'm a more interesting person when I'm working," they say. The guidance counselor, psychologist, physician, social worker and writer were still working as were the unmarried.

With the younger girls (pre-adolescents) fear of death may also represent a retaliation anxiety to the death or loss of mother as expressed in their TAT stories. In the mature group, there seems to be a higher commitment and altruism. But they appear to be less intellectual than the young adults, or the mid-adolescents. Most are in the generative stage, as expressed in wanting to help and care for the next generation. Generativity manifests

[160]

itself also in productivity and creativity in work, in guiding the current youth. Only about half of the women appear to have reached this stage; a few seem closer to the negative pole of stagnation and are too absorbed in themselves to care about others. The mother who has stayed at home and concentrated an overabundance of energy onto her two children often reacts to their leaving home by feelings of desertion: such women harbor a devastating void in their lives. One has been drinking heavily, another uses poor health to keep her daughter nearby and apart from her son-in-law whose work takes him far away. Others develop new or revive old interests. At this period the subjects are usually free to exercise their own choice. There are more options; subjects are guided by the tyranny of what others think, and financial return assumes less importance.

In the integrating of identifications with important strivings, capacities, interests, values and roles, particularly work roles, many of the pieces of personality become reassembled. In a few the stamina to translate these into action is weak. Yet there is palpably grater cohesion and substance than formerly. The group divides approximately into half who tend toward the positive pole, and half toward the negative one.

To sum up the dominant direction of the changes and progress in the stages: in order to reach maturity, the boy has to make peace with his father image, and the girl with that of her mother.

In the days after adolescence or what Erikson calls young adulthood and Blos post-adolescence, and which is also clear in my data there are continuous efforts to come to terms with the ego interests and attitudes of parents. The energy can now be transformed into stable sublimations. The incomplete solution of the phase-specific task can be endured for a while; it is likely to flare in parenthood usually in connection with the child of the same sex. But at this period social institutions and cultural conditions, also superego components, and marriage as well as society help the young adult to become more firmly

[161]

anchored in his society. At this period, instinctual conflicts recede into the background and the integrative processes hopefully take over. An analysis of these involves a search for steps in the repetition compulsion so useful in working with the student on a synthesized vocational direction.

# CHAPTER 13
## Counseling Discussion

After filtering through and pondering over this wealth of material related to developmental growth, the message is clear: age and time do make a difference in the formation of an identity, both personal and vocational. So, too, in large measure, do the individual's family, its structure and emotional climate, the quality of the transactions among family members, as well as the degree of sensitivity of the child's role model or identification figure, both early and late. Not only is this true of family members, but also of peers, and later key figures at work. We have also seen the influence of the teacher and the school. Chronic illness in the family leaves its mark in extremely stressful relationships and at times slows up the subject's development. This seems to happen especially when the ill parent is hospitalized or when a sibling with an irreversible illness dominates the home. The concept of the developmental stages and the particular tasks of the Erikson stages clamor to be used and the book is replete with illustrations via the case histories.

*An example of the effect of illness on family dynamics*
Lou at 14 jitters about in her chair as if she were ready to "take off" in flight. She is a tall, slight girl, tense and anxious. Like her mother, Lou has been ill periodically with the same chronic disturbance for which mother has been hospitalized frequently. The illness started when Lou was a baby — a rare medical history. When mother is in the hospital, Lou takes over in running the home which she shares with her father, a chain store executive, and her older sister who is now at college. The beauty of sister is constantly emphasized. "She is much prettier than I am."

Again like mother, Lou is gifted musically: she both sings and dances. But she will never consider becoming a performer because her profession would take her away from home and make it necessary for her to leave her children. So she expects to marry right after college and have four or five offspring. "I am determined to be with them all the time." To safeguard this plan, she has already discontinued her music lessons which she loves. So far in her occasional talks with a counselor, Lou refrained from mentioning alternate possibilities. Then she announced her acceptance of another choice of her mother— going to kindergarten school and becoming a teacher, "so I can fall back on it if I needed to earn my living." This, too, is mother's recommendation. Despite Lou's real strengths as shown in handling a difficult situation, her tendency to overidentify with her mother makes it less likely that she can develop her sense of me-ness and be herself. Now she displaces the blame onto her mother who was upset at the mere mention of Lou becoming an actress. Her confused, ambivalent identifications increase the complexity of resolving the triangular situation, for father is playing mother's role and the situation is heightened by the unusual arrangements at home. Lou cannot aspire to be like her mother or to rebel, for mother is ill and suffers considerably. To be like mother exposes Lou to constant danger. So she identifies chiefly with young children, kindergarteners, who are safe and protected. Teaching kindergarten children will allow her to play a mother role involving closeness and giving but also the children are encouraged to be independent and to grow. And she can use her gifts for piano and song in her work while feeding her own unmet nurturing needs and dependency. In her current stage of young or early adolescence, she identifies also with her peers and enjoys them. There are indications of potential strength in Lou's high intelligence, her rich fantasy life, and her ability to reach and express her feelings. In two TAT or fantasy stories, she rescues her dying mother. But in

[164]

actuality she is forced to play roles for which she is not ready. The pace at which subjects move ahead gives a rough index of readiness in general — a valuable concept in counseling.

Erikson usually uses the generic term "adolescence" — in a few instances he specifies "late adolescence" which is the way we have interpreted it. But communication of reseach results would be more meaningful if the generic term were broken down and reported in more precise terms — early, mid-, late, and post-adolescence. It is clear that the young adolescent at 14 and the late adolescent at 19 or 20 are totally different girls. Alleviating a problem which is obviously phase-specific should be scheduled for counseling at the time of that stage and should be regarded as less serious or characterological. I have aimed at delineating the growth of identity over a period of critical years and at studying the reciprocal relation between the identity and the relevant occupational attitudes and behavior. In arriving at this relation, application of understanding of the force of the repetition compulsion and the coming into awareness of the nature of the conflicts which the counselee is trying to master provides an orientation which points a direction as the girl talks of her aspirations and ideals while the counselor listens for patterns of repetition which may be significant. The group's statement that they want to meet in order to understand themselves better augers well. As observed in the group meeting the younger subjects did not respond with enthusiasm to the discussion of future occupations. With prior identity counseling, however, they might be more responsive.

A considerably shortened test battery slanted towards identity formation and work role could be devised for large-scale use. It could be geared to instruments which are adapted for use in groups and are repeatable, such tests as Machover Draw-a-Person, a worker, an ideal; a specially constructed Identity Sentence Completion Test; and handwriting analysis which has the added advantage of being easily available. Included in this

[165]

section is a suggested use of case studies. Early memories and the Pigem Test, too, are effective evaluative tools which are not time-consuming. Four pertinent TAT pictures might be included; they can now be computer scored.

Confidence in oneself and acceptance by important others can be *consciously fostered* by teachers and counselors in the everyday goings on of school life; many perceptive teachers and counselors try to build confidence intuitively through use of selective praise. It also applies to parents if the acceptance is genuine, and not tinged with anxiety over occasional deviation from what other parents do — a weapon which some teen-agers wield in exploiting parents. Nor need parents worry that the imposition of reasonable controls may cause a neurosis when basic relationships are sound. Often children *want* boundaries.

Some mothers are aware of the changes that have taken place recently, and interpret these as the prelude to the adolescent storm. Too few mothers, about one in four, react with more modulated attitudes toward typical adolescent behavior. These women have come to grips with their own identity problems, and possess egos that help them cope with the environment and tolerance for expression of impulse, together with a comfortable conscience. They were flexible enough to change with their daughters. Hence they can empathize with them at periods of crisis and are not overwhelmed by reactivation of their own earlier pressures. Moreover they try not to thwart the thrust toward autonomy in their daughters. Through the years of 11 to 14, fathers refer to the girls as "just babies"; it is hard for them to conceive of the girls in adult roles. Many of the girls wish that their fathers would give them advice; others seek more attention from them. Most mothers, however, encourage their daughters to seek a professional role rather than marry early as they had done.

When mothers have occupations (and only a few do), their work is mostly at a professional level.

[166]

The literature in guidance emphasizes the biological impact on adolescents. I have recognized this influence but have focused on the psychological counterparts; often both interact. When talking with 14-year-old girls, one after another, the apathy and sheer depression stir one; and when this is accompanied by falling grades and fantasied stories on the TAT featuring death of the parents, it seems likely that the subject equates this loss with that in her reveries and dreams. This suggests the intensity of efforts to free themselves from the control of the home.

In a few years when they are approaching mid-adolescence and are considering college plans, such feelings moderate and fade. I meet them in the corridors and find their moods again cheerful. The agents of change seem to be not only the home, school and community activities, dates with boys, intense friendships with girls, but above all, the support of the mother, the girl's new stage of development and her ability to fulfill its task. In the group meeting, the counselor might stimulate discussion of a pertinent case which would serve as a springboard to attitudes toward self and their place in building an identity, as well as an illustration of a particular point. Alternatives to marriage *or* career could be discussed, marriage and part-time career, or politics, or club work, or resumption of earlier interests, such as music, ceramics, or other art work. With prior identity counseling, the almost mystical belief that career diminishes opportunities for marriage might be clarified.

Should my findings be substantiated, it would seem that the focus of counseling of girls ages 11 through 14 should dwell more on their attitudes toward the kind of future life they want in the form, perhaps, of group discussions concerning the lives of women who have had a variety of activities. What would you want your life to be like after you marry? How many children do you want?

Many teachers who serve as positive identification figures throughout the school day can contribute to self-esteem and other attitudes toward self wherever possible; many teachers do this intuitively. Kindergarten teachers mention characteristics which still prevail in the subjects. They are skilled observers; perhaps the absence of the influence from prior opinions contributes a freedom and lack of bias. Decisions as to whether or not teachers should be included as active co-leaders of groups requires further study.

Were it possible to schedule meetings for parents, counselors could attempt to bring to discussion whatever concerned them, whether it be falling grades, underachieving, overdependency one minute, too much independence the next, moods or the concept of the developmental progression. Many parents of seniors seem to be overconcerned with admission to the Ivy League colleges and expect their daughters to have chosen a field; but this is a rare occurrence. Experimentation will be needed on the most efficient size of the group, and its relative economy. The former approach is ongoing at some secondary schools, junior and senior colleges as well as at graduate schools. Important also would be a comparative study of how girls at other age levels respond to group meetings with an identity emphasis. Our subjects were at an age when they were drawn to girls and therefore well motivated to participate. Counseling sessions held in a group on a biweekly basis, along with one or two individual monthly interviews might be a starting point.

Decisions will be needed as to whether individual or group counseling or both will be the preferred method. Our young adolescents at 14 were unproductive in the individual interview but lively and full of ideas when with the group. This phase of adolescence was chosen because friends and peers hold intense meaning at this period, and seem to support the members to speak more freely and thoughtfully.

The Blos formulation and that of Erikson can, I believe, be adapted systematically to the field of counseling. So, too, can the self-concept theories of Super (1955) and the possibilities of sublimation and influence of early experience explicated by

[168]

Nachman and Segal (1960) and others, especially the premises of Roe (1959). My own findings on the interpenetrations of identity formation and occupational choice and the capacity of one to alter the other, offer another point of departure. My efforts to make explicit the "stuff" or components of this mutual exchange, offer to the counselor an organizing perspective, a way of looking searchingly at the counselee, for a work goal which has personal meaning to both counselee and counselor and which they explore together.

The joy of developmental counseling is its relevance to life experiences, insight into self, and what Maslow calls peak episodes. This includes decisions about college and the experiences there which usually mean being on one's own; the settling on a life style as well as a life work; the choice of spouse and the rearing of children. All of these need to be systemized according to age and stage. Blos and Erikson have contributed richly to these tasks.

Another concept of great magnitude revolves around identity as a precursor to self-counseling. In these days of shortages in available counselors, self insights on the counselee's part can partially, but not wholly, fill the gap. The negative factor would be a curtailing of the counselee-counselor relationship of such supreme value. But this relationship could be continued on a reduced time basis with the counselor available for difficult situations in the counseling process. Moreover, such a schedule would free some of the counselor's time, for she needs to become a human relations specialist which will probably entail additional study. And the counselee who can learn to understand her occupational potential can also learn to grasp broader areas of her emotional life such as, for instance, her reaction to boys. The counselor can help the student extensively with aspects of integration and consolidation in building an identity rich in understanding, insight, and empathy — all of vital importance in decision-making. As with other cognitive efforts, there will be individual differences in performance.

[169]

# CHAPTER 14

The Reciprocity Between Identity and Occupational Choice

The clue to understanding can emerge quite tentatively at times with a single unusual statement. In Pat's history (Chapter 5) she tells us in response to the Pigem Test that she wants to live and work in a protected setting characterized by permanency, that she fears life's transience. Her response to the Pigem asking what she would want to be were she to return to life but couldn't be human, was "Sand — it would always be there." This and other emphases on continuity suggest an intense fear of death and strong need for protection and safety. So, too, in her discussion of possible occupations she selects teaching. In this connection, she speaks of the "steady stream of children — some one will always be there." Here Pat stresses the cloister-like atmosphere of the school setting. These may symbolize life eternal; they may serve as an antidote to her anxiety about death. Her life experience is laced with incidents of sudden death.

What Pat may have been communicating is on a less than conscious level. But it is the language often spoken by counselees. The counselor needs to be able to grasp its meaning, although she would not interpret it to the subject. It takes us a step closer to what may be the basic dynamic in a particular choice, and as such clamors for understanding and recognition in helping counselees to make a meaningful choice.

*Example of one use of case material*
In teaching a seminar for counselors, the author arranged the histories into two parts — a format which separated the background data from the interpretations, then removed the

latter from the folder. After reading the history, each student tried her hand at formulating a hypothesis pertinent to a broad tentative field for the subject. Later when the interpretive material was returned to the students, they again tried to order and make sense of the data. Here they concentrated on the dynamic thread running through the material. This led to a lively, meaningful discussion with considerable disagreement which the students tried to resolve. The actual choice provided the criterion. The seminar resulted, I believe, in enhanced insight and empathy — the sina quo non of counseling. We have used other material, too, as a springboard for positive discussions.

Components of empathy and insight are part of the counselor's essential work kit. By clinical sense, I am not referring to pathology (some counselors use this meaning) but to the concept of ego synthesis and the achievement of wholeness, unity and cohesiveness of the ego, or the reverse, a fragile sense of self.

The degree of similarity and correspondence between the developmental data and dynamics presented by Erikson and Blos and the personal and vocational attitudes of the subjects is gratifying.

*Significant values*

Just five subjects introduced the topic of the individual's responsibility for what happens to her: a single and astute preadolescent, two mid-adolescents and two young adults.

Few subjects spoke openly of their antagonisms towards parents in general, or of their anger when parents pushed them towards a certain occupation or away from one which they had tentatively selected. The projective test findings were, however, permeated with rage over the coercive tactics of parents.

Many of the subjects assumed attitudes which suggested that occupation was something outside of their orbit, a phenomenon

[171]

that comes about through others. Even throughout adolescence, they reacted to the prospect of marriage as if they were worthless without such status. Their degree of self-confidence revolved around the occupation of their future husbands. My findings reinforce the view expressed earlier that the individual is both agent and reactor to the positive and negative pressures of her life, as well as to her way of dealing with these pressures. More specifically, her reactions show the quality of her coping mechanisms and defenses — an area in which a good part of the individual change took place. Compromise, counteraction, perspective and reality testing are positive defenses; denial, rigidity, projection, displacement, and somatizing are usually more primitive.

I am not implying the need for familiarity with pathological nosologies but to the way "normal" people try to solve their dilemmas and defend themselves against strain and anxiety, for it is in *the defenses and coping mechanisms* that most of the changes in our subjects have taken place. The more advanced coping mechanisms feature suppression rather than repression, detouring around rather than meeting the anxiety-stimulating event head on. In counseling, reaction formation in choice of an occupation is frequently used and its effectiveness usually depends on the strength of the impulses. The team approach would be helpful in implementing such a plan.

No mention has been made of the factor of remuneration as a motivating force in occupational choice. Certainly this factor is prominent in only four of the occupational biographies. Some of our subjects are using their incomes for their husbands' graduate training. From another study in which the author is currently engaged, the point of view on remuneration seems partially associated with socio-economic class. Those with high family incomes and upper or upper-middle class status, tend to work at non-salaried activity if at all, and/or are preoccupied

[172]

with art and music or club work but not as a paid vocation; only a few give high priority to salary.

Of prime importance is the way that an adaptive occupational role increases a general feeling of competence and contributes to toughening the identity formation, while this in turn bulwarks the occupational role involvement.

The time in history through which the subjects live affects overall identity formation as does the state of the economy. The parents of the younger girls grew up during the "great Depression" when one's best efforts to find a job were of little avail. This was especially disenchanting to the young high school or college graduate with no experience, the situation of most of the parents; *they had lost control of their environment.* Fathers, brothers, even a son of one of the mature subjects had participated in the wars: World War II or Korea or Vietnam. Two were wounded, one killed. Another, a father, was away for four years. Social, technical, political storms and changes have run rampant throughout the lifetime of the subjects, reminding one of the old-time movie projectors which operated at such rapid speed that the total meaning of the film was blurred. The uncertainties, traumas, and especially the impermanence — all can be "caught" from the parents if not self-experienced. Historically, the last two decades may have tended to slow up the development of an identity or distort it.

How *are* lives shaped? This question has been the subject of an inordinate amount of study by White (1969). In his fine book, *Lives in Progress,* he expresses the conviction that not one but many forces mold us: the sociological, biological, cultural; also the occupational, educational and psychological. So pervasive a question is it that related topcis are affected, and it reaches many issues basic to members of the Women's Liberation movement, who believe that the differences between men and women are minimal. Reverberations reach even the cosmic question of whether or not anatomy governs destiny, and has even spread

[173]

in hushed tones to speculation concerning the effect on women, should artificial insemination ever be used on a large scale. The Movement's emphasis on our being what is taught us revives the age-old issue of nature versus nurture, and in a sense that of the value of *general* versus *specific* abilities in learning. Are we born that way, the product of our genes? Or have we been indoctrinated by family members and teachers? It is only a step from discussion of biological influences and that of psychodynamics of a particular personality. My smaller problem is to consider the psychodynamics of the work situation with emphasis on special gratification because of the reciprocity and mutuality between personal and work identities.

Freud dominated the field for many years and still wields an enormous influence in the biological but also the ego areas. He is not accepted by the feminists because of his biological emphasis and because of his alleged belief that man is superior to woman.

*Psychoanalytic and psychodynamic aspects of work theory*

Neff *(Work and Human Behavior,* 1969) has reviewed and put in order some of the above theories, a few rooted in psychoanalysis but all in his opinion psychodynamically oriented. The question is no longer who you are, rather it is what you *do,* and with what coping mechanisms. The child brings to the school his unique ways of behaving as found in both built-in as well as in imprinting on the part of the family, classmates, and calibre of teachers. The girl's achievement in school usually regulates the place of achievement in her life.

The sizable number of individuals coming to a psychiatric clinic because of disturbances in work escalates further each day. Freud leaves his readers with the impression that the more important aspects of personality development are concluded by the time the child is five or six, and at the third or phallic stage of development. One of Erikson's crucial periods is that of

[174]

*Industry* around age 11 in which the child first begins to develop his attitudes toward work and achievement. But Erikson by no means downgrades the earlier years of childhood; he regards them of major significance. Certainly the growing child must first meet and resolve problems of weaning and sphincter control as well as jealousy problems.

Hendricks has put forward the thesis that there is a work principle which governs the operation of the executant functions. "He posits a mastery instinct as the source of the energy." Barbara Lantos, a psychoanalyst, has written two papers on work (1943, 1952). She makes the point that play and work are distinguished not by their content but by their purpose. Asking why feelings of independence, freedom and security are pleasurable, she points to the connection in most people between work and the ability to guarantee one's existence. She sees pleasure in work achievement as an ego rather than an id principle. But she feels with Freud that men do not work spontaneously. The motive is self-preservation "mediated by intelligence, and reinforced by conscience." (Lantos 1952) Like Erikson, Lantos feels "that the transition from pleasure in activity to pleasure in achievement takes place in the latency period." One is an outer force (necessity) the other is inner . . . internalized aggression in the ultimate guarantee of the maintenance of work and of self-preservation. To quote Freud, the "ego has set itself the task of self preservation." Obendorf's papers on work hew more closely to orthodox psychoanalysis in which there is an over or under investment in work directly associated with relationships with parents. The concept of sublimation is generally emphasized by most theorists.

There seems to be an increase in the instances in which work is no longer the central axis of life. An important factor in this revolves around increases in automation of the industrial revolution in which the worker moves further and further from participating in the completed product, and deriving pride from

[175]

work. Some workers resort almost to depersonalization in handling this situation when severe. Young people have observed that affluence does not add up to parental happiness. Why, they ask, should they work as hard as their fathers do? Why not coast along at graduate school? Neff (1969) speaks of some of the strains on identity of our complex society. Yet occupation is a most potent force in integrating and cementing identity. In primitive times, the individual was a member of a given tribe, a kinship group, and a family. Beliefs and customs and functions were carefully prescribed. There was little if any confusion of roles. The worker had a name known to others, a lineage, an extended family, a clearly marked status — all guiding important actions in his life. He had a place to live, different from our sprawling urban sections. Neff feels that the school represents to the child his first venture into society, even though he brings with him strong familial and pre-school influences. There is a trend suggesting that the more skilled and prestigeful an occupation, the more formal education it requires. The pattern seems to be set in the early school years, but only as a progression from infancy, stage by stage, to the school years and the vital concept of industry as an ego value.

Lantos feels that Hendricks goes too far in assuming a work instinct whereas Obendorf hews closely to the traditional psychoanalytic line. The pleasure in work is a consequence of gratification of the instinct to master the environment. Gratification in man must be worked for: it floats into the ego where it becomes desexualized and deaggressivised or "neutralized" in Hartman's terms.

I find that drive reduction theories regarding work are in eclipse; that the competence and effectance ideas of White tend to be escalating.

The difference between health and pathology is not always in the presence or absence of deep conflict; it is often in the patterning and balancing of conflict and resources. Some of the "normal" girls have many of the dark themes on projectives that we would expect to and actually do find in the protocols of a seriously disturbed group, but these themes are counterbalanced and contained resources such as intelligence, special talent, strong ties, by intact and concerned families and above all, by the urge to master difficulty. The relative strength and intensity of the drives stacked against those of the defenses also makes considerable difference in the functioning of the individual.

Some of the roots of the conflict in women's identity and its relationship to occupational role have been suggested. Our society views identity in men and women basically in terms of sex role. In men sex role is generally enhanced and strengthened by occupational role; in women, on the other hand, sex role is sometimes confused by occupational role. Society presumably backs this situation in order to protect and insure the biological functioning of women.

To the ego, the past is not an inexorable force; it is part of the present effort to resolve difficulties. To repeat one of Erikson's points (1959) possessing particular significance for counselors: The characteristic and much publicized disturbance of adolescence is *essentially determined by the life task of the particular stage, and is most readily ameliorated during the very stage of its development. . ."* If the outcome for some of the subjects seems cloaked in gloom, this may be because of the particular stage (as in young adolescence) which often arouses depression, apathy, and the sense of loss characteristic of breaking home ties. Critics misinterpret what they think is an enduring personality disturbance but according to Erikson is usually a transient upset which manifests itself one year, but has moderated the next.

Though mentioned by two precocious early adolescents, more young adults expressed the somewhat profound attitude that the individual is usually responsible for what happened in her

[177]

own life; that at times she "asks for" her own particular brand of heartache. Fear of aging and death were mentioned by a few mid-adolescents; it was understandably a more general theme for the mature woman. A few of these are returning to the employment market or have recently resumed their profession after years at home. Their high degree of altruism and commitment are notable.

One would expect that mid-adolescents, usually seniors faced with the need of choosing either a job or college or specialized training would be hungry for help in considering possibilities. But this clashes with their need for independence. Late adolescence, quieter internally and more ready to draw their lives together, have an advantageous position on the counseling timetable.

This book has been built around the basic principle of counseling. A description of the total process has not been intended. I have been able, in view of the limitations of space and the overall planning, to touch on only the significance of the relationship between student and counselor. Yet this is of overwhelming significance; it is implicit in the stories the subjects tell of their life experiences and aspirations.

Each counselor develops her own work style based on a particular rationale and on the sort of person she is. Hopefully, this will include a fundamental belief in certain overriding principles, such as the dignity of the individual counselee in being able to make her own decisions. Communication between student and counselor hinges on what the former wants to do with her life and rests essentially on her shoulders within the limits of reality. First of all the relation is that of a human encounter. Later, after a relationship has evolved, the message of the counselor is that what the student decides matters a good deal to the counselor who will help. Such an approach must be genuine, for students are alert to and condemn the "phony." The word "caring" has been bandied about too much; it seems, however, to fit here in describing some counselors.

Above all, the counselor specifically needs to be effective as a listener, a catalyst, a challenger, and an identification figure — one who acts as a stimulus to realistic planning and synthesis of courses, work values, and style of life. Add to this load some of the other functions of the counselor, such as giving, scoring, and interpreting tests, personality and interest inventories, etc., writing college references, attending many meetings, referring students to other sources of help, collecting occupational information, taking some administrative responsibility, seeing parents. When, then, does she have time for counseling? When does she find the months and years required to increase the skill and specialized knowledge necessary for understanding human behavior and getting the full value of meaning which the child or student is trying to convey? Little seems to be done on a systematic basis about follow-up data, from which we could learn.

Many in the counseling specialty believe that the core of the process is to help individuals open the door to their identity, personal and vocational, and to a growing inwardness and awareness of self. I trumpet out the lofty value of such an aim — one which I believe will maximize integration and minimize the inner dissonance of individuals searching for job gratification.

# PART III

## The Women's Liberation Movement

# CHAPTER 15
## The Women's Liberation Movement:
## Its Psychosocial Dynamics

The focus moves now to the identities of the members of the feminist movement — identities which seem to have shifted as the movement has mushroomed. Its looseness of structure imposes organizational difficulties to the chronicling of its growth. I will try to convey the atmosphere of the meetings I attended and the climate of the women in their sit-ins, marches, and demonstrations, some of which I observed, as I did some of their rap and consciousness-raising sessions. Even more revealing were my talks with about fifteen Women's Liberation members, randomly selected, whom I attempted to rate according to their developmental status on the Erikson Stages of Ego Development and comparison with another group, the young adults described in the early part of the book. This material will be reported later. What I am attempting here, however rough and tentative, is to present aspects of the *psycho-social* dynamics of the movement.

No one seems quite sure of the size of the Lib movement founded in 1966 by Betty Friedan after women showed an enormously positive response to her book *The Feminine Mystique*. The size has been reported as ranging between ten to fifteen thousand, more by now. The National Organization for Women (NOW) constitutes a large part of the movement, and claims to have 300 chapters throughout the country; it is still the senior group. Their aims and activities have emphasized legislation, both new and that which has never been enforced, such as sex discrimination in employment. They have worked hard and effectively for more day care centers. But their overall aim seems to be to have husbands share domestic responsibilities, to counteract male chauvinism and make their own decisions as well as gaining equality in participating in decisions. Freedom is their cardinal aim. Members have also worked hard for more liberal revision of birth control and abortion laws.

In addition to NOW, there are many other sub-groups, such as one called Bread and Roses, which publish news letters, demonstrate, and dramatize their beliefs. Among other techniques, they use a chant "Better Dead than Wed" — the effect is that of a Greek chorus. Members of this group regard themselves as radicals; their political base is the Socialist party. Another sub-group teaches Karate; the Red Stockings and New York Radicals both have an extremist political base. To compound the confusion, there is intense in-fighting. Polarization seems to be based on how wild or establishment-oriented the groups are.

The history of the feminist movement has been written so often and so well that I see no point in repeating it here. But a word is needed to link the earlier section of this book with the present one. Lib members took the lead in recognizing the relevance of slanting vocational counseling toward prestige occupations, and have specified this as an important plank in their platform. They write: "Vocational counseling in high schools and colleges should be totally oriented so as not to channel women into low pay, low prestige jobs."

Such an aim is implicit in the philosophy of the earlier part of the book: that the counselor and counselee search for clues to the particular fields which offer rewards and gratifications consonant with the counselee's personal identity. One needs the relevant qualifications for a prestige job. Such counseling allows for the harnessing of the power resulting from the mutuality of personal and vocational identities.

Concomitant with the development of the movement, the long, futile, cruel Vietnam War adds to the general malaise of

[184]

people today, chipping away at morale and leaving a diffuse rebellious quality which seems world-wide. Yet a dedicated cadre of women have found their voice, strident and shrill though it may sometimes be; they use these voices vociferously and often effectively against inequities presumably foisted on them by men — the oppressors and tyrants. For what stands out in the behavior of the members is their furious, venomous hatred. This is referred to as male domination or chauvinism. But there seems to be none of this frenzied hatred of men in the young adults, or comparison group formerly presented as central to Group III in Parts I and II of this book. This will be presented in more detail later.

The activities of the Liberation group consist of general monthly meetings in which members discuss whatever is on their minds, or have a speaker, or practice consciousness-raising. Much of the activity takes place in small local groups. It was hard to get from the members an articulate statement as to just what consciousness-raising means. To this writer it seems to be a blend of group dynamic techniques, sensitivity and encounter training plus a confessional, round-robin procedure aimed at a heightened awareness of the part men play in the nub of the feminist problem.

The negative criticism of the movement directed chiefly toward the violence of their tactics. To understate, Lib members are accused of being too action-oriented — such action as physically ousting a publisher from his desk and later from his office while they shrieked raucously. Members are also accused of being obsessed with sex. This is documented by some members' absorption in the controversy as to whether the clitoral or vaginal orgasm is more effective.

It must confuse members to be told by Dana Densmore — a Lib leader, that sex is not essential to life and that we are programmed to crave sex. In a pamphlet, "Sex Roles and Female Oppression," Miss Densmore writes: "Unlike man, who

[185]

is the doer, woman is the sustainer, she is not permitted to actualize her human potential. She is a purely biological creature living in an alien world she did not make. The creation of new life takes place in her body which is being *used,* she nourishes the infant there. Similarly she sustains her man, nourishing him by preparing his food. Men, then, do not see child-bearing as a burden . . . but the liberation woman asks why she is required to stifle her abilities . . . and *play a role defined by men for the benefit of men?* She lives as a parasite, and only through the man . . . who has set things up because this is the way he likes them.

"Any woman who dares to reject the role . . . is accused of being neurotic, and trying to be a man. Because of the stigma attached to rejecting the feminine role, women who know they are miserable in it deny the allegation because of the implications people draw. Basically she doesn't want to be a woman, they say. On the other hand, if a man isn't attracted to her, she is accused of being an old maid, a lesbian, a man-hater, or frigid. When men recognize shortcomings in themselves, they feel they are unmanly and inadequate. The result is a constant effort to *prove they are men.* The female provides them someone to feel superior to and to push around."

In "Sex and The Single Girl," the same author deplores the effort that some women make to beautify themselves in an effort to find romance. "Never mind that your plain unvarnished self would not have landed him at all. When women stoop to conquer they relinquish all rights to respect later . . . declare themselves traditional role-playing women who delight in their own degradation. Psychologists (male) have defined you as a creature whose ego development demands a delicate balance of narcissism and masochism. Why should you like being dominated by man? . . . He isn't being virile and manly, he's showing disrespect and disregard for you. Virility is a euphemism. The real word is sadism.

"If we are ugly and plain, men demand that we do something

[186]

about it. One does not offer a woman a chance to show by words or actions what her personality really is. Men adore you for your appearance. But if you are brainy, it will be taken as quaint. It is rare to read about human beings instead of brains and beauty and fragments of individuals."

Dana Densmore drops one of the final bombs in the chapter "On Celibacy." She says: "One hangup to liberation is a supposed need for sex . . . which is not essential to life as eating is . . . We are programmed to crave sex. It sells consumer goods, gives a life in a dull and routinized world. It is a means of power to women. But we must come to realize that sex is actually a minor need. Erotic energy is just life energy and is quickly worked off if you are doing interesting, absorbing things. Love and affection and recognition can easily be found in comrades, an open love that cares for you for yourself and not for how docile and cute and sexy and ego building you are, a love in which you are always subject, never merely object. You, who have had such heady ability to charm and arouse . . . must be willing to give it up . . . and reject the false image that makes men love us and then men will cease to love us."

In the section "On Sisterhood," the author asks: "Do you see yourself as strong, more able to resist or reject conditioning, act as an individual to a greater extent than others? It is because you were fortunate enough to have some countervailing influences that others didn't have. Perhaps you were more trusted by your parents . . . or you were taught certain values and learned to trust yourself and your instincts.

"We are all one. All the same influences have acted on us. If you have escaped the consequences of your conditioning, you are lucky, not different or superior. We are all sisters. Yet there is an incredible lack of compassion, explainable only as a defensive rejection to avoid identification, for successful career women tend to identify with men. The concept of sisterhood perhaps creates an affinity among members, a bond which tends to moderate isolation and motivate expression."

A thread of insight into some of the dynamics of these beliefs shines through. Apparently many of the women have been exposed to men who do need to prove their virility, and who are searching for a mother symbol in their choice of spouse.

Dana Densmore speaks of female ego development as dependent on a delicate balance of narcissism and masochism. Yet this insight is not congruent with the Liberation program. Even the avoidance of beautifying techniques plays havoc with the image of self, an important ego value.

One wonders about the effect of some of the suggestions in the pamphlet should they be carried out. Basically, the author seems to be saying "women do not want to be women." She mentions an attempt to escape from identifications. But positive ones are precisely what are needed. For many of these women do not know who they are. Whatever identification figures they have had are not integrated or blended into the personality. Some of their convictions about the roles of men and women are encapsulated and have not been subjected to reality awareness. In discussing the subjects of Lib, they use somewhat primitive defenses — displacement, projection, denial, and acting out. What these women do have now is such a strong sense of group identity that they overidentify. As one views them in the group, many impress one as lonely people, for whom the movement probably represents group belongingness, and the opportunity to play roles, but underlying the loneliness appears to be anger and frustration. It is the social area which produces gratifications abundantly.

The ideas relating to celibacy as stated in the pamphlet would seem to be an interference with nature, and with what may be the essence of living for some. Further it violates the perpetuation of life and has dangerous implications. Its treatment in the pamphlet follows the material against beautifying oneself and

[188]

eliminating romance. The dictum is that one must be loved for their essential selves — stark and unembellished. Further, it is a bit chilling that there is no mention of the effect on women who truly *want* children.

If there has been a change in identity, similar changes in identification figures should precede it. Perhaps the identification with the movement partially supplants that of the individual. If the identification with the group is an *over*identification it dilutes the positive effect of the group identity.

It is difficult to make general statements about the movement because the element of homogeneity in the NOW chapters does not carry over in the other sub-groups, especially the more radical ones. The writer herself is plagued with vacillating feelings about the organization as are others. Parts of the program are admirable and long overdue; parts seem a bit frenetic and more serious, lacking in a theoretical base. It is a religion to many. Some of the members must have mixed feelings, too, about leaving their children, and about the expression of resentful attitudes toward husbands. In the give and take of conversation, one would expect some focus on how offspring might be affected. But few if any references to children were heard. Certainly the subject of child care centers is allied. How will they be staffed? With what quality of personnel?

The hyperbole used by a portion of the liberation group — "women are slaves and victims; men are oppressors" — seems over-determined as if the meaning came from the age-old antipathies, the perpetual vendettas between men and women rather than the immediate surface irritation. There is a mounting or cumulative effect which reinforces an earlier feeling, vague though it is, of being shortchanged by life. Many of the women are truly obsessed with the movement. Why, I wonder, did they refrain from doing something about the brain-washing before? Their attitudes toward selves are maudlin, and savor of "poor, poor me."

[189]

In an article called "The Golden Rule and the Life Cycle" (1963), Erikson defines mutuality as a relationship in which partners depend on each other for the development of their respective strengths. It evolves from infancy and is marked by the stages of basic trust versus mistrust. Erikson suggests endowing the Golden Rule with a principle of mutuality, replacing the reciprocity of prudence and sympathy. He continues;

"I cannot leave the subject of the two sexes without a word on the uniqueness of women. They are being granted [some] equality of political rights and the recognition of a certain sameness in mental and moral equipment. But what they have *not* begun to learn is the equal right to be effectively unique and to use hard won rights in the service of what they uniquely represent in human evolution. One senses today the emergence of a new feminism as part of a more inclusive humanism. This coincides with a growing conviction, highly ambivalent to be sure — that the future of mankind cannot depend on men alone and may well depend on the fate of a mother variable uncontrolled by technological man. The resistance to such a consideration always comes from free men and women who are mortally afraid that by emphasizing what is unique, one may tend to re-emphasize what is unequal. Study of life histories certainly confirms a far-reaching sameness in men and women insofar as they express the mathematical architecture of the universe, the organization of logical thought and the structure of language. Such studies also suggest that while men and women think, act, and talk alike, they naturally do not experience their bodies (and thus the world) alike."

The concept of anatomy determining destiny is anathema to many of the Lib women. Cultural and environmental conditioning are what count, they feel. The effect of parental expectations that girls should play with girls in girls' activities are first steps in grooming for marriage and motherhood as the only way of life. This, they say, accounts for the differences in the behavior of boys and of girls. Kagan, Erikson, Bettelheim, Spock, and Harlow, to name a few, have documented biological differences which we see every day in variations in height, weight, strength, temperament, etc. Both biological and environ-

[190]

mental determinents can operate. In the brain-damaged child her perceptions seem to be distorted and this makes her more vulnerable to the development of schizophrenia, thought by many to be the result of pathological family interaction.

I do not want to minimize the power of the environmental influence. Up to the time of graduation, mothers urge their daughters to achieve and to be somebody, perhaps partially because the parents unwittingly want to use the child to be somebody themselves. When one girl broached the subject of continuing in graduate work, her mother reacted negatively. "Do you want to be a blue stocking and wall flower all your life? Put on some makeup and get yourself a good husband. Forget about more study." This shift in the attitude of the mother confuses the girl and her sense of identity. To have some choice is the right of every girl. While acknowledging the influence of the environment, I affirm and recommend the inclusion of psychological factors inherent in anatomical differences.

## CHAPTER 16
### The Status of Men in the Movement

Were men welcome at Lib meetings, I asked one 22-year-old member. "They should have their own meetings," she replied. "Ours feature sisterhood which they couldn't understand. We are utterly frank with each other; none of us play roles inflicted by men." But she seemed unable to define "sisterhood."

The following are some of the guiding questions that flooded my mind in trying to understand the movement.

1. Do the Lib groups have a special lack of tolerance for discrimination and deprivation? When later frustrations are built onto a superstructure of previous pressures, the cumulative effect is often overwhelming.

2. Does such low tolerance particularize in their attitudes toward men? Why?

3. Does work mean more to them than to others in the sense of showing what they can do in the world outside? For when the spell of the pay check fades, many women prefer to stay at home before a cozy fire in winter. Frequently they talk of wanting to work if they could find the right job, but do little about getting one.

4. Do the Lib women have a stronger-than-average need to be recognized and appreciated? Do they want to be loved for themselves alone, the essential self, stripped of all embellishments? Is this why they defeminize women?

5. What is behind the upsurge of the intensive rebellious feeling at this point in time? Is the movement partially a revolution against a sick society, similar in some ways to the black and youth revolutions? There are many more questions which can

be answered only on the basis of detailed background information which we lack.

6. But one more: Have some of the members always been independent thinkers, generally negative, or mavericks? Is there a sizable element of the characteralogical? Has either parent been involved in causes?

I have a few web-like impressions (and they are only that) about the questions listed above. But the material will need replication on larger samples. My hunch, backed up by a few facts, is that the members do seem to have a somewhat lower threshold for deprivation than most. *Rarely* do they say that their fathers or brothers responded to the movement with a display of interest. There is the suggestion that fathers show a rather cool affect in general. And men personify the chief target of the liberators. It is generally accepted that the father is usually the prototype of the daughter's image of the male. A large percentage of women had younger brothers who may have dethroned them symbolically so that there is a basic over-sensitivity to discrimination or deprivation already established.

*Possible identities of a group of Lib members*

These seem to be for the most part a highly intelligent group of women, ambitious, high-key and attractive with quick, active minds. I think, again most tentatively, that the women have a greater than average need to show what they can do, to get out in the world and feel part of it. But they need generous rewards. Aside from the activity and socializing which accompany the movement, the response and/or appreciation for their efforts are significant. This may be related to the early deprivation, or short-changing. My reaction to the last question again tends in the positive direction. Two said, "I've been a feminist all my life."

I do believe that the "sick" society contributes in part to the dismal tenor of the times, the disillusionment, the malaise, the feeling of alienation following the disenchantment with the leadership and quality of the politics of the country, the gaps in communication, as well as inconsistency and hypocrisy in some of the examples set by parents on a world-wide scale. Some members apparently have a low tolerance for such a society and become ill.

My informants were vague in explaining the role which Sisterhood plays. It seems to connote warmth and support and humanism, all bulwarking the ego. The need to belong and derive added strength is important. On a less conscious basis, the sister concept may be a mother symbol counteracting the hunger gnawing at many of the women. More than this, the courage to confront one's self honestly is a pillar of identity. For when acceptance by other members who continue to like you despite the unfolding, as the ideal sister does, the result is a positive, strengthening one. Individual members recall that they too had a similar experience, and the confessor feels less isolated. They are all cut from the same cloth; it is the pattern of what they make of it that matters. One member said: "Now I don't care what others think and do. I'm concerned with what's right for me."

It seems to me that many of the Lib women underplay occupation. When I asked about their job hunting, the subject was sloughed off and discussion terminated. Instead of stating qualifications, they tended to indoctrinate the interviewer with Lib shibboleths.

Only during the last fifty years or so have such large numbers of women worked outside of the home. Yet it is often through work that we fulfill our identity. According to Carlyle: "Blessed is the man who has found his work." It is an aspect of life which can bring gratification through the use of mental as well as back muscles. In his description of the Protestant Ethic, Weber has pinpointed the significance of work as a device for assuaging guilt. Perhaps this applies to the millions of jobs in

[194]

mass production where there is minimal exercise of skill or ideas and less fulfillment than frustration. An occupation or career which is satisfying on the other hand builds and reinforces ego functioning. The hippies avoided work; one would expect this to have heightened rather than reduced guilt.

Attitudes toward women range over the spectrum. Contrast what Erikson has to say about their uniqueness and potential value to society, with the opinion of Thomas Aquinas and Aristotle. The former says: "A female is something deficient here by chance only"; the latter: "Women are characterized by a certain lack of qualities. We should regard the female nature as afflicted with a natural defectiveness."

Many women in the Liberation movement want to work, need to work, and would probably find gratifications through work especially congruent with their personalities. This will be possible only with the availability of more child care centers, and a large proportion of the membership aim their efforts in this direction. The next obstacle in the course is sex discrimination in employment which lowers their earnings and their morale. A further hurdle is the conviction held by the members that successful career women are imitating men. This tarnishes their status with the movement.

Lucky women may have that plum, a part-time job, even if they work as little as one day a week. A social worker friend says that with five young children at home her one day a week job gives her a chance to catch her breath and relax, besides the opportunity to use her mind and see and talk with adults. Because some women take jobs which are convenient, near home, with good hours and a good rate of pay so that they can buy a few extra things for the house, they make slow progress. There is little authentic challenge in the nature of the work. The ambition to put their children through college offers more substantial motivation.

What follows is an overview of the content and rationale of

[195]

one of the monthly meetings for all factions. I had brief talks with about thirty of the varied members of the sub-groups. This, together with the reading in the field, watching plays, T.V. and radio series, as well as attending meetings, contributed to my impressions of the members.

I am using the word "identity" as distinct from role; the latter is conceived of as the expression of personality in action. Shifts in the girls and women are more apt appear in roles rather than identities. Certainly the bulk of liberation women are underplaying or overplaying roles which have changed from the meek mouse to the angry lion. For if they abhor men and mistrust women, who else is there? There are, of course, the children who appear to be lost in their activities and in the Lib literature. Are they an albatross around the necks of their parents? When day care activities are being discussed, one hears no mention of how the individual child may react to possible weaknesses in the program personnel.

Liberation women have their hands full dealing with their day to day problems and attending meetings as well as rap sessions. I have been told that their schedule often calls for three meetings a day or during a single evening. I hope they don't get so bogged down in their current dilemmas that they lose sight of some of the larger implications of the movement in its potential and possible leverage value. Larger problems exist in how this strength can be woven into a fabric of greater scope — the overall problem of humanism which transcends the immediate and the here and now.

An important finding is that Women's Lib does not represent all women — even the majority of them. A recent Gallop Poll reported that 65 per cent of respondents polled disapproved of the organization and had no interest in joining. Only 3 per cent of college students are members. It would seem that women in the lower classes are not attracted to the movement, whereas middle-class women flock to the meetings. The former — lower

[196]

class — appear to accept and even seek the domineering male. Many middle-class men tend to be somewhat passive rather than chauvinistic. One of the chief complaints of men crowding the psychiatric clinics in the colleges is concern over impotence.

Lib rationale seems largely based on Locke's *tabula rasa;* differences among people are rooted in anatomy, parturition, and gender.

That some women, like men, have a strong drive to do something with their lives or to make their mark, is often ignored. Ambitions of families are directed primarily to their sons and to the mythical man the daughter may marry some day. Should the daughter complete her graduate work and gain professional status, the chance of her continuing at it are higher. Until parents learn to encourage their daughters as well as their sons, waste of talent will proliferate.

The characteristic uniqueness of women heightens the difficulty of clustering them into groups with a common base. But I have also been impressed with the huge discrepancies in the attitudes of the Lib women and those of the young adults at the intimacy stage. The differences center directly on attitudes to men and family.

At times a group identity of moderate dimensions substitutes for identifications with individuals. For certain individuals can cope with groups effectively while they lack the capacity for close relationships with people. Or some can play successfully the role of wife but fail when the role of mother is challenged.

Roles serve the purpose of a bridge between the inner self and social functioning. Action is clearly implied. When the roles are consistent, enduring, and germane to the personality, they provide a means of adapting. But it is when one plays too many roles, some ego-alien, that role diffusion sets in and the identity may become fragmented.

The individual identity, on the other hand, derives from the older, earlier and more substantial traits. During the tumultuous

[197]

identity crisis of adolescence — early and middle — the crisis can be integrated and modified if the individual personality is not too rigid and unyielding. Some of it is absorbed in the construction of an occupational identity, for it is the inability to settle on this which disturbs individual young people, according to Erikson. Once this is determined, however tentatively, the identity is firmed by social identifications, work, marriage, family, and above all by firmer personal identities, as well as feminine ones.

Moreover, the individual identity must derive from an integration of a selective assortment of identifications, hopefully a repudiation of negative and a strengthening of the positive ones — all absorbed by and kindred to those of the girl herself. As Erikson says, it is more than a sum of childhood identifications; "It is the accrued experience of the ego's ability to integrate all identifications with the vicissitudes of the libido, with the aptitudes developed out of endowment, and with the opportunities offered in social roles. The sense of ego identity, then, is the accrued confidence that the inner sameness and continuity of one's meaning for others is evidenced in the tangible promise of a career. The danger of this stage is role diffusion."

To repeat, a lasting ego identity cannot begin to exist without the trust of the first oral stage; it cannot be completed without the inner sameness supporting the sum of childhood identifications and matched by the sameness and continuity of one's meaning for others.

Two of the radical sub-groups limit their membership to 30 per cent of married women. A feminist was heard to say: "I have come to view married members as a built-in self destruct." This *mistrust* of other women and in turn the attitudes of some women, non-members, toward the movement highlight a weakness. I am referring to the reluctance on the part of some to change their way of living. Independence frightens them: complacency and the status quo are what they cling to.

[198]

Nonetheless the movement has snowballed to an extent which suggests that the reluctance to join on the part of some may subside after the new ways are more generally accepted. The liberation movement, however, is young and enthusiastic. Some of their statements could be accepted were there some qualifications.

*Have the identities changed?* Perhaps to some slight degree their self-images have shifted, and some reorganization has taken place. The projective or displacement defense, blaming the husband, has been displaced onto men collectively. What is really remarkable is the power of the group identity — the alliance with the movement. This has cemented the members together into a cohesive sense of belonging.

Recently members have complained about male ogling of women. Irritating though it may be, greater dignity might result if a similar amount of time were spent on larger, more vital issues, such as housing, medical care and medical costs to mention a few. If women can hope *only* for sex gratification her essential overall relationship with a man may still be empty and barren. She can, it is true, develop a sex role identity, but her more cosmic identity as a human being and a woman may be stunted. With the aid of sublimation, a rich and comfortable vocational sense of self, there is potential for filling in some of the gaps, so that she can live a fuller, yet discriminating kind of life.

I am writing this phase of studying changing identities not only to acquaint individuals interested in social phenomena with the ongoings of a feminist movement, but also because of my own feeling that beneath the day to day activities, eccentricity and occasional bizarre behavior lie some unused identity components. Their absence lowers the use of what may be excellent work potential. On the other hand it is apparent that a high degree of togetherness directed toward a cause has resulted in exacerbation of yearning for togetherness which membership in the movement has nurtured, and which seems particularly gratifying to members.

Except for the options of part-time work or rotating with husband on a time schedule, the full-time worker must carry a backbreaking load. Actually she has two full-time jobs. The advent of the four-day week may modify her hours; and the move for population control could tend to reduce the size of families, making life simpler for working wives, many of whom work because they need to. Another possible aid might be the conveyance of ideas and "how to" information on women establishing businesses of their own, preferably with a partner who can share the hours which the work requires.

How had the liberation movement helped her? I asked one member. Her response: "It has made me feel like more of a person." She had always enjoyed debating and speaking at college. But since then she had had to spend most of her time at home with the children (four) doing the mundane household chores. At the meetings, Alice tends to throw out provocative questions; she is articulate and plays the role of the gadfly. The members listen to her, especially to her tirades against men. Occasionally she tends to be somewhat impulsive.

Identification with her western friend, a Lib member who visited Alice at a time of uncertainty, appears to have clinched her decision to join the organization. The status permits some displacement, also some sublimation. Men are the chief target of the movement, and Alice can transfer her obvious resentment toward her husband which recently mounted to crisis proportions, to this larger group, the Lib movement. Certainly the marital relationship is a precursor to her enthusiasm for the overall conviction concerning "man — the oppressor." But there is much in the agenda of the movement which is gratifying to her now that she is freer; her children are now in school or in a day care center.

The members impressed me as a lively, friendly group, high

[200]

voltage in temperament. The atmosphere is informal since only first names are used. There was a scattering of men and the members soon surrounded them while a few stayed at the periphery with their own small group, as if masculinity were out of their orbit.

The meeting room was crowded and noisy as with most large gatherings. There was some giggling and a slight hysterical note. Most of the talk seemed to center on the subject of Lib and its wonders. My seat neighbor continually complained that the meetings always started late. She wore a hearing aid.

The Libs were casually but modishly dressed on the whole. The speaker, a member of one of the sub-groups, repeated again and again the many injustices plaguing women because of sex discrimination in employment.

## CHAPTER 17
### An Overview

As a publicity project, the sub-groups of the movement combined in programming a twenty-four hour "marathon" radio broadcast dedicated to clarifying the fundamental convictions and ideologies of the movement. Questions from the audience were answered by a panel of Lib women. It is difficult to cluster these, for the replies reflected the sub-group with which the member was affiliated. The uniqueness, however, surpassed the similarities. One homogeneity is the intensity of the interest and the degree of investment in the movement.

Via radio a few members who I hope are not representative gave answers that were impulsive and unrealistic; they seemed to want to shock the audience with their off-beat view of sex. Men were attacked throughout. Investment in tactics super-ordinated that in strategy. At the other end of the continuum were a few Lib women who spoke in calm, modulated tones, were highly educated and disciplined thinkers. The type of questions they drew was also different; they dealt more with ideology and the intellectual phases of the movement. These members were working primarily in the legislative and task force ends of the program. Although they, too, had met considerable frustration and deprivation in their careers, they seemed able to accept and absorb it without embitterment and displacing all of the blame onto men. (One had her doctorate in theology, but because of regulations, could not be ordained as a minister, a profession confined to men in most churches.) These women seemed less absorbed in the movement than in their private lives. A rather small percentage were married and mothers.

[202]

In between these two extremes fall most of the members. Some might be classified as the "silent majority." Here one finds the bulk of the married women whom one might chat with in a supermarket. They seem especially responsive to the practical values of the program, such as the day care centers which will allow them to return to work. They say that they feel "itchy" from staying at home too much. They need more activity than Lib meetings provide, although the increased social life is welcome. There appears to be less of the frenetic in their manner.

But I was amazed at the amount of frenzied rage in the voices of some of the callers to the radio station, both men and women. Feminism is a charged subject it seems! Except for the first group described above, the Lib women accepted the tirades rather objectively, were not overdefensive. The majority of men who called were polite but a bit amused and patronizing by what one called the "belligerent antics" of the members. He was referring to their demonstrations and sit-ins. Members emphasized their high regard for the movement but were again inarticulate in discussing reasons for this veneration. The leaders, in contrast, are quite articulate. But is easier to single out weaknesses than to produce remedies, especially for what some regard as defects in society and in basic customs, both of a long standing nature. Betty Friedan is now recognizing the need for the cooperation of men to survive and grow. Moreover her long-range goal is to use the movement as a springboard to politics.

The general effect when they were together at activities reflected the role playing behavior which was so prominent. This was also apparent at the anniversary celebration. The Libs wore suffragette uniforms with bloomers and amusing labels; there was even a drum major, a huge woman, and the group broke out in one of their chants from time to time. As one would expect, their orientation was more masculine than feminine. A more structured and definitive identity takes place after role

[203]

experimentation. The counterpart is role confusion, the category into which a fairly large proportion of the Libs fall on the Erikson scale. Bisexuality often accompanies such behavior. If, however, those with a dramatic flair could be given opportunities to formally dramatize these roles, sublimation might be a partial result.

I think of roles as personality expressed in patterns of behavior in contrast to the infinitely greater durability of identity. Unfortunately I have slight comparison data on the role playing activity of the young adults. There was, however, variability among the Libs themselves which should be studied further. They seem also to be performing the role of the rescuer of women, the crusader, but also from a positive veiwpoint that of the realistic woman who wants her rights, deserves them, and is willing to work for them.

It is interesting that the Women's Rights Group many years ago waged a battle against intemperance and promoted trade unionism. In "The American Female," *(Harper's* October 1962), the editors advised women to examine their roles as members of the human race in addition to being wives and mothers. This is what is going on today. But according to the **Harper** editors it is happening privately and with such an unmilitant air that few know about it.

In the interests of accuracy and objectivity, and as a switch, perhaps one should mention a single advantage of women over men. Responsible as they are for the support of the family, men do not have as much latitude as women for investigating job opportunities in a range of fields, nor can they afford to be unemployed for any considerable time.

But one of the more puzzling planks in the Lib platform is that fostering defeminization. "Abolish Sexism" is their slogan. They advocate cropping the hair, abolishing make-up, and the ritualistic burning of brassieres. Navy fatigues constitute popular battle dress, especially among members of Bread and Roses.

*Playboy Magazine* and its Bunnies are taboo; the fact that men make money from women's bodies is hotly resented. To women who want to be loved for themselves, they say such things are degrading. They are angered when a group of men whistle at them. A growing hunger for special affection seems to be a central core of their identities, but they feel that they must deny it. Image of self lags and needs nourishing but the rewards are rare. In the nature of their clothing and the banning of cosmetics, their constant use of four-letter words, some of the women seem to be imitating the very men they hate, a common coping mechanism. What identity they have is a negative or ambivalent one; the latter confuses the member, so is tantamount to no identity at all.

The dilemma of differences in skills between men and women has long been a debatable one. Any one who has taught in the primary grades is pretty certain that girls and women surpass most boys and men in verbal skills. Professor Kagan of Harvard has been researching this and other aspects of sex differences in ability for some time. He believes that there are subtle differences in cerebral dominance and that little girls respond to auditory excitation, boys to visual. The earlier the sex difference in behavior appears, the more likely it is to be genetically determined. This author in working with infants found that girls are more alive to social stimuli while boys show more mobility and aggression.

I have advanced the thesis that some of the hatred toward men may stem from unfortunate episodes with males in the earlier years of life — perhaps from a negative relationship with father and/or jealousy of a younger brother who usurped her favored position in the family. And I am wondering what part the attitudes and behavior and identities of the husbands play. Some appear to be quite sophisticated and may be aware of the truism that if he treats her like a woman it will foster her femininity. By this I do not mean her prowess in the kitchen.

[205]

Rather do I have in mind the mutuality that Erikson speaks of. Perhaps the husband senses that the rotating schedules of working hours proposed as a solution or other part-time combinations will fail to serve the real purpose of solidifying his wife's femininity. Hence he may be resisting these plans and dragging his feet in sharing the responsibility for caring for the children and the home. With the exception of the oedipal, pre- and young adolescence, up to the beginning of the late adolescent stages, identifications with mother are largely negative and ambivalent, especially the latter. There seemed to be some reluctance to talk about this parent; and emotions are labile in the mid and latter parts of these developmental stages.

When trying to explain the fascination that Lib holds for their members, only a few women specify tangible, concrete results: "I have more confidence now. I can ad lib at meetings and even preside without shaking." Another: "Now that I've day care facilities I get out of the house more which makes me more cheerful." A third member said, "Now that I have my Lib friends, we go everywhere together. My life used to revolve around boys whether I liked them or not." Some of these young women in their early twenties had worked with SDS while in college and since then for some of the civil rights and peace organizations. A few were currently working for the Lib movement on a part-time basis. Many lived in communes. Formerly they worked under the supervision of men, but soon realized that they were being given the less desirable jobs, so formed their own units. These young women claimed to have no interest in men or marriage. One, however, told me in the interview that she loved children. The tenor of the group opinion was that anyone can be a mother.

Earlier I expressed the hope of learning more about the boundless motivation of the Lib members, their enthusiasm and commitment. These forces probably include belief in the aims of the movement to the point of making them a "cause." Perhaps they also derive enjoyment from the active social life involved, which gives them a reason for getting away from home, for many seem like lonely, frustrated, restless women.

But the intensity goes further; it is like a mass contagion with a touch of self or group hypnosis and hysteria, so heightened is their suggestibility to the ideas of the leaders and fellow members. Resistance to the movement comes from a women's group who hang onto the status quo of their daily routine, and are fearful of change; others are so dependent on their husbands that they truly want to be told what to do. The bond between them seems to be great in many instances. Still other women cling to the prestige of the mother and housewife role.

With a portion of the Lib members, role experimentation and a more structured sex identity failed to take shape. The counterpart is role confusion which at times leads to a bisexual orientation, according to Erikson. This may be what is operating in the manner in which many women imitate men in their modes of dress, their use of four-letter words, and their militant behavior — while simultaneously attacking everything masculine. Ambivalence reigns in their sex identity.

I wonder whether the member who said, "I've been a feminist since age three," would remember this episode had there been no other reinforcing agent. Her brother was born when she was approximately three or four, and at the vulnerable oedipal stage. This boy may have been the target of her jealousy and anger at being ousted from her place in the sun which she held as the only child. Is he the small version of the men she hates — a hate which is flaring and heightened by the serious troubles with her husband? Can we lay it all at the door of male chauvinism? It is interesting that in the group of fifteen Lib members, ten had younger brothers, the young adults had only *four!*

When the author, with Ernest A. Haggard, wrote in 1948 a monograph called *Work Adjustment in Relation to Family Back-*

*ground,* the mutuality between the personal identity of the individual and her work horizons intrigued this writer, who thought then that it could be explained on the basis of the repetition compulsion. On further exploration the link in question seemed to be serving the purpose of mastering or conquering troublesome hang-ups dating back to an earlier age. Blos calls them "residual traumata" and feels that they are universal.

It's time to take a closer look at the raging hatred for men which permeates the movement. Even this seems to be moderating according to Friedan's recent remarks. Happenstance or not, there seems to be a greater-than-average incidence of divorce among the Lib women. The national ratio is one in every four, while in the group being studied, it is close to one to three. A few others with whom I talked were dissatisfied with their marriages and had frequent thoughts of ending them. It would seem that the antipathy for men pre-dated its current expression.

Bits of autobiographical information have appeared in the growing literature about the Lib movement and some of its leaders. In the article in *Time* magazine for August 30, 1971 titled "Who's Come a Long Way Baby?", Kate Millet tells of her hatred for her father who beat her and walked out on the family of three girls. Kate was the middle child. This happened at age fourteen when attachment to father is usually at its height, and when he is the model for other men in her life. "I'll never forget it." Father of three girls, he was angry with the all-feminine offspring and disparaged their gender. Surely this father has contributed to Kate's current conceptions of men whom she denigrates. In Part I of this book, the father is consistently the favored parent of the girls. This does not seem as definitive in the Lib group. And the early lives of Friedan, Densmore, and Ti-grace Atkinson are fraught with unhappiness and parental conflict. I hope that the reader will remember that there is a large component of speculation in the attempt to reconstruct lives when data are so skimpy.

Many of the Lib members deny their individual identities and go all out for group identifications. One strong identification is with the suffragettes. A comment such as "I've been a feminist since I was three," makes one ponder. Would it be remembered all these years without some reinforcing experience? This family configuration may partially explain the vulnerability to being deprived or even worse, dethroned. With the exception of those garbed in navy fatigues, blue jeans and sweaters predominated at the monthly meeting. A few wore pantsuits or afternoon dresses.

Almost a third of the women I talked with were introduced to Lib by Betty Friedan's book, *The Feminine Mystique,* others through *Letters to the Editor* or through friends and classmates. A few repeated such comments as: "I've been waiting a long time for this." But they did not articulate or elaborate these statements even when asked. They were not quite clear about the specific factor of the movement that appealed to them. Nor did they elaborate on the nature of consciousness-raising or the role of the sister in the functioning of the overall work.

On the other hand, some preferred chapters with a more radical ideology hoping to change drastically the system of marriage — perhaps abolishing it. I believe that Kate Millet is in accord with this. The meteoric thrust of her remarkable book, *Sexual Politics,* seems to be shifting to reverse.

When Freud made his well-known remark about love and work on being asked what a normal person should do well, his intent was to include a general work productivity or experiences of inspiration from teachers, according to Erikson. Other characteristics of the young adults are delineated in Chapter 9. The task at this stage of intimacy is to grow psychologically through motherhood and wifehood. Danger lies in failing to achieve the developmental milestone at its approximate time, delaying arrival until the stage of role confusion. Some of the Lib members, it would seem, are still uncertain as to who they are and where they are going. They play roles for the benefit of others instead of experimenting for themselves, going out of their way to use four-letter words wherever possible. With some such identity as they have derives from males.

The prominent activist member, Kate Millet, has made academic progress which has been extraordinary. For this she deserves great credit; she did it the hard way. Extensive, too, is her knowledge of literature. But is she fluent in genetics, in logic, biology, and sociology? Robert Fox, the Rutgers anthropologist, says: "Millet's theory that gender is imposed by society is a typical half-truth. Masculine and feminine roles are reinforced by families but this does not deny the existence of genetic differences, those which appear to be built-in in infants."

Blos writes: "Fixations provide the specificity of choices in terms of libidinal needs, prevalent identifications and favored fancies. Residual traumata furnish the *force* [repetition compulsion] which pushes unintegrated experiences into the mental life for eventual mastery. The direction this process takes, has its emphasis on sublimation and defense — through identification and the form is influenced by environment, social institutions, traditional mores, and value systems."

I have used this approach with a satisfying degree of effectiveness, and hope to adapt it further to counseling and communicate it to others. Blos has already provided more than the first step.

As suggested before, many of the Lib wives pressure their husbands to help more with the housework and to share responsibilities for the children. Resentment of this on the part of husbands is probably communicated to the children. Even in the evening, wives attend as many as three meetings in a single night after working all day. Husbands accuse them of thinking, talking, and living Lib, all day and night, and losing interest in

[210]

their homes. Said one: "I didn't slave at law school for three years to be a baby sitter each afternoon." The number who do cooperate is, however, a sizable one.

When role confusion, the stage of a fair number of the Lib women, is based on strong previous doubts of sexual identity, delinquency or psychotic episodes are not uncommon, according to Erikson. This is the time of clubs and cliques to which loyalty surpasses that to parents — a period reminiscent of young adolescence when girls are absorbed with meetings and cliques duplicating *current* behavior at times.

Erikson goes to the heart of the matter when he writes of uniqueness as a prominent characteristic of women. They put their own particular stamp and signature on what they do and say. But the Lib women appear to be less singular than the non-members and control group of young adults so far as their activities within the movement are concerned.

Recently I read that the Lib movement in a large German city had set fire to and destroyed a bridal shop. Is this an expression of hatred for women, more particularly those who marry? A speculation: one is reminded of the quota set for admission of *married* women by one of the New York City Lib groups. No doubt there are complex reasons for their action which reach to those across the ocean and suggest the world-wide aspect of the rebellion. Self-hatred seems to be part of the development, as is clear in the Densmore pamphlet. Does the bride symbolize beauty and freshness and the admiration the members love but lack — as a contrast to defeminization? Do the mounting negative identifications with the beautiful ones, the married ones, and of course men themselves leave them in limbo — with large amounts of energy tied up in the hatred and frustration so prevalent?

Who does speak for women? Not the 65 per cent or less of respondents on the Gallup Poll who oppose the movement; or the dependent ones who cling to the status quo. Primarily

[211]

women speak for themselves with uniqueness and singularity, their special traits. But we have seen how a relatively small group of energetic, hard-working purposeful women have made themselves heard despite minority status.

The audiences at meetings listened rather passively to the perseverative speeches, voicing no disagreement. Nor was there any real discussion of the issues consisting of variations on the theme of men being responsible for the dire circumstances of women.

Kate Millet calls for a cultural revolution; she wants to change society which must necessarily involve political reorganization. She bases this on her strong belief that differences between the sexes follow the indoctrination pattern. It is Germaine Greer's firm opinion that marriage should be abolished. No antagonism for men motivates this feeling, she claims and is less "carried away" than some other leaders.

I mentioned earlier that women that I talked with at Lib meetings tended to avoid discussion of or even refer to children. This is apparently a concern of Janet Malcolm, writing in the *New Republic*. "The frightening issue she raises is this: from feminist writings one gathers that the claims of children are incompatible with the rights of women, and that it is the children, being the less important of the two, who must be sacrificed." Moreover in the data I gathered from the developmental groups girls continued to favor their fathers over mothers through the late adolescence.

But the cutting edge of the criticism comes from an article called the "Feminine Mistake" in *Esquire* (January 1971) by Helen Lawrenson. It would seem that she has caught some of the frenzied fury of the Lib women. She speaks of their work as "manipulated hysteria," calls them "sick silly creatures." It seems to baffle her that the movement is growing nonetheless. Again she says: "These are not normal women. I think they are freaks." These are statements that would be difficult to document even though some of them may be partially true. Such epithets however do not apply to all of the women. What Lib loses sight of is that many women enjoy household tasks if they have some time free and away from home. "Most women have a strong nesting instinct." The last statement is backed by a New York organization called Pussy Cat League whose members oppose the Lib movement and who profess to like things as they are. Must we all have uniform opinions?

Apparently the Lib women have been slower in developing roles that are relevant and which they can integrate. While they are overidentifying in their "all out," indiscriminate devotion to *everything* in the movement, the strength of their clique which served a positive purpose earlier in adolescence may compensate for some of the alienation in some of these individuals. Group solidarity could be a key factor. If it is true that a large proportion are particularly lonely people, the movement may serve as therapeutic togetherness.

I spoke earlier about comparing the Lib members with the young adults according to the Erikson stages. From quantitative and clinical viewpoints the differences between the groups are sharp. *None* of the young adults expressed the fury toward men which we hear from the Libs. Actually they voice a distinctly reverse attitude, wanting to share in all of their husbands' experiences and activities even to the point of working with them in business. There are differences too, in relationships with children: the Libs give the impression of a remote quality in contrast to the closeness and warmth of the young adults toward their children.

A few reminders about the young adults who make up the comparison group:

*The fifteen young adults in the stage of intimacy vs. isolation* comprise the one group whereas an equal number of Lib members make up the other. Erikson comments that the young adults, emerging from the search for identity, are eager and willing to

[213]

fuse their identities with those of others, and are ready for intimacy or its counterpart, isolation versus distantiation. If he or she can face the fear of ego loss in situations that call for abandon, in affiliations, orgasms, sexual unions, and in close friendships, chances are there will be smooth sailing. The danger of this stage is that intimate, combative, and competitive attitudes are both with and against the self-same people. But as these are integrated, they eventually become subject to the ethical sense which is the mark of the adult. Again, the danger of this stage is isolation, the avoidance of contacts which commit to intimacy. There are partnerships which amount to isolation à deux. By and large, however, the hatred of men by the Lib group would negate the positive attitudes of the young adults.

Many items on the movement's agenda are admirable and badly needed. How to implement them equitably and according to a *theoretical framework* is the real challenge. Both the half-time job option and that worked out in six-month alternations, with men and women spelling each other, one staying at home for six months while the spouse goes to work, are replete with snags. If, as many economists say, we are facing serious unemployment, the time will not be ripe, for the need in such an event would be for the recruitment for enough jobs to go around. Moreover, such arrangements tamper essentially with sex roles and with defenses built up to cope with anxiety and with tension. That is why skilled experimenters are needed.

Dr. Kardner, an anthropologist who has studied many primitive cultures, feels that the monogamous one is superior and that it is imperative to have the child with the mother for a continuous period of time. In contrast, there are advantages to communal living. Many years lie ahead and experts such as Margaret Mead and Talcott Parsons both feel that the movement is *the* problem of the decade.

Vivian Gornick in an article in the New York *Times* of January 10, 1971 has written on consciousness-raising, describing the reactions of a group of women who are not in the Lib movement although they participate in some of their activities. The author of this article regards the technique as an effective approach to the movement and the most celebrated introduction for a feminist conversion. She defines consciousness-raising as the feminist practice of examining one's personal experience in the light of sexism — that theory which explains women's subordinate position in society as the result of a cultural decision to confer direct power on men and only indirect power on women. The implication is that men made this decision rather maliciously.

If one accepts all the way the priority of cultural determination over, let's say, the biological, and also the belief that we write our own biographies, the above falls into logical line. But there are thousands who do not accept this. Consciousness-raising differs from group therapy, for the Lib people have no leader, nor are fees involved. The absence of any semblance of a screening device for admission to groups such as these, and also the encounter groups, flashes a blinking light to those in positions of responsibility in group work.

Perhaps the author's experience of sitting in with a consciousness-raising group may clarify the procedure. A list of possible topics was circulated, such as love, femininity, work. The group chose one titled *Why I Married My Husband*. Of the fifteen women around the table, only two mentioned love as the reason. There followed a discussion about whether love and sex were equated by men but the women failed to come to any definite conclusion. Love, most agreed, included genuine liking for a man, for his convictions, integrity, etc. The trouble is, said one "I don't really like my husband very much; nor do we enjoy the same things. On coming home for dinner, the TV is on constantly tuned to *his* favorite programs, not mine, and he pays no attention to what I might enjoy. What he wants is sports, sports, sports." The other members of the group echoed this statement: "I married him because I liked the man I thought he was but not what

[215]

he actually is." At this point she cried and the members expressed sympathy, adding their agreement with the member's question: "Isn't it better to live with a man and learn what he is really like before marriage?" The situation was interpreted in the light of male chauvinism. Other group members thought that they had grown in personal stature while husbands had not. A serious young woman said that she had "asked for" her dependent relationship with her husband. Hence she thought she should make an active effort to become more independent. She had been in analysis for five years.

What I hoped to learn was whether these data could be roughly but meaningfully sorted into two disparate groups using as variables these data on which the subjects had been studied. I ranked them, using the time schedule of the Erikson stages, to indicate whether ego development seemed to be "on time" or "late." I aspired to the approximate only. It turned out that all but two of the young adults were *on time;* two appeared to be somewhat *late.* (There were fifteen in each group). Lib bulked in the stage of role confusion — one stage earlier and at the negative pole. *Ten Lib members clustered* within this negative stage while five were approximately on time. Twice as many of the fifteen subjects who were the young adults had met their tasks according to schedule. Such a difference reaches statistical significance. This is an oversimplistic way of grouping the data, but it can be refined later if useful.

I hope I won't be misunderstood to be implying that the Lib group is inferior. What I am saying is that the groups *differ.* It does seem, however, that there has been a slight lag in development which may disappear or moderate when subjected to synthesis at the way stations of growth which still lie ahead.

Members and their followers form sub-groups which polarize according to how "wild" they are. To compound the confusion, in-fighting abounds.

There is a small group of members, often those who have been recently married, who object vigorously to the blame which is directed toward men. The enormity of the problems of women, and their potential were they allowed to be individuals and to have periods of freedom during their daily routine, surpasses in importance the real dilemmas of their relation to men at this time. For whatever men have contributed to the problem, it was not done maliciously, and may obscure other more subtle issues.

Husbands, some contend, are sympathetic and genuinely interested in the movement. Why should they be maligned? Other husbands do time-consuming chores for the organization. Although men are reported to be hostile to the movement, they help with Xeroxing and such chores as vacuuming at home when asked. Whether or not this will survive the honeymoon, I do not know. They seem to have little fear of change which they can absorb without a struggle. What the proportion of cooperative spouses is among the movement membership, I do not know. Were a more extensive survey being made, precise statistics should be available. This would of course call for a tighter organization but the reward and potential of such background information in understanding what is going on and where to go from that point are enormous. The role of the husband in the liberation group is still a mystery. I try to visualize the husband-wife relationship of the sub-group of the broadcast I described earlier, wives who to me seemed to have strident, abrasive personalities. I must hasten to say that of those I heard this was a small unit. It seemed clear that many of this sub-group are perennial man-haters. How then do their husbands function at home? Do they identify with their wives as a means of self-protection? Or do they buck and fight? Perhaps they work late at the office to escape the friction. How do they react to their children, and what sort of relationship do the member and her husband have? Chiefly, we hear the man damned; is he ever praised? How about his self-esteem?

[217]

It would seem that only a handful of members has changed outwardly to a discernible degree. They may have one or two more free days a week, but they are far from liberated. One of the largest gains seems to emerge in the form of exhilaration and the protection that the movement provides; also the social life. But there are also suggestions that more women are now holding jobs formerly given only to men. And legislation is now making strides. Ideas are being expressed in interesting books such as the *Second Wave*. There are a spate of such books.

Interestingly, the change is in the sense of personal worth. "I am more of a person now." Members have made themselves felt though their identity is still forced at times. They are now editing books and magazines *on their own*. They are able to speak before a group more effectively. As a result they no longer need to channel their anger onto men.

I have the impression that enthusiasm for the movement has become a bit forced in some areas; the excitement is over. The larger question is: does the movement have the strength needed to survive the pressures and weaknesses in the integration process? And how can this be bulwarked?

In *Life* Magazine for August 1971, there is a reprint of an article by Mrs. Chapman Catt, the suffragette, totalling up the price of the early-in-the-century victory. President Wilson finally capitulated but two more years of work were still needed. In all, there were *the equivalent of 52 years of campaigning,* 56 state referenda campaigns, 480 drives to get state legislators to submit suffrage amendments; 317 additional campaigns for suffrage planks, and 19 campaigns for the 19 congresses. Said Mrs. Catt to her followers: "The vote has been costly. Prize it." Have they done so?

The male liberationists refrained from displacing the blame onto women. They are objective and mild. The first men to accept the stand that women are right in their convictions; they quickly, perhaps too quickly, acknowledge the shortages in

[218]

their own behavior. "With women there is an oppressor. Their enemy is men. But our enemy *is not women*. It's the *role* we are forced to play." Norman Mailer, who knows his way around in social and political arenas, seems intrigued with the Lib movement, and reacted after considerable study of their issues in the March 1971 number of *Harper's;* its title, "A Prisoner of Sex." He replaced the usual term "penis envy" with that of penis fear in referring to male sexuality. Elizabeth Janeway, in her excellent book *Man's Power and Woman's Place,* affirms this fear and urges that women pay attention to it. Mrs. Janeway has traced the history of the Lib movement through the use of age-old myths and legends to illustrate how male-female attitudes developed and were absorbed over time. Her book is a carefully researched one, scholarly and perceptive.

What these men seem to want is a state in which they are totally fulfilled sexually. Quite a few speak of female partners, not wives. "We see nothing wrong with honest other relations." Their attitude seems passive, even masochistic, tending to lean on women, at times exaggeratedly asking one to take over in putting in a car battery or repairing a dishwasher. But in this branch of the Lib movement, they have joined women instead of fighting them. Perhaps they are acting out their chief coping mechanism, passivity. Housekeeping is the subject which they find hardest to discuss.

In the same issue of *Life* Magazine there is an article by Barry Farrell on the present status of the Liberation movement for both men and women. It penetrates to the essential shortage in the movement; that is the absence of accurate images of the men involved. For women do not live in a vacuum; they are also wives, mothers, housekeepers, wage earners, executives. Just as we now treat the emotionally sick child in the context of the sick family, or as a unit which is constantly interacting, so, too, should we study the woman problem as part of the man's dilemma, and vice versa. Until both are more liberated,

[219]

there will be minimal freedom for either. A woman can achieve a good degree of liberation with *one man but not with another*. It might be more productive to study women only or men only; but also mixed groups.

It is the woman's image of her son as the All-American he-man that women have been identified with; they berate themselves for this stand. As the author of the article presents the situation, men recognize their overconcern with their maleness, as well as the corresponding responsibilities which express themselves in numerous sexual fears, as Norman Mailer has suggested. "The struggle to live up to the impossible standards of virility has made them strangers to themselves and their own feelings about each other." Men were also dismayed by the new ferocity of their women.

Women have a precious tool in their inwardness and openness to insights. May this gift be sustained and hopefully proliferate. Some members complain that they are caught in the squeeze between the life style they want for themselves on the one hand, and on what society expects of them on the other. By the term "society," I include community, neighborhood, school, and family. A sizable segment of non-members ascribe a rigid role to their sex; it consists of staying at home and caring for the children. If these are combined with a few outside activities, it appears to be tolerable for a woman whose identity is closely entwined with that of her husband. But numerous members have an image of themselves based on a higher degree of self-actualization. They have good minds which have been well-trained and they want to use their capacities, as well as to grow as individuals.

The word "guilt" resounds among the members. Should they return to work, what will they do when their children are sick, they ask? In actuality, this seems to be a fairly rare occurrence. But I do not know the answer to the working mother's question. I do know that she must learn not to panic, to make emergency arrangements in advance, and to depend more on her husband who in this particular circumstance worked nearby. He was able to come home at frequent intervals. Whereas day care offers valuable growth experiences to many children, it may not work well for others. Discrimination in selecting students is vital; day care may not be geared to the child with exceptionally strong dependency needs, and weak coping mechanisms in handling the abundant anxiety of a strange environment without the support of her mother. Many day care workers are making a fine contribution in relieving the pressures experienced on the laden working mother. Others hold onto the old way of life, perhaps staying at home and rationalizing their decision. But taking a firm, considered stand which a woman feels is wise and positive, and staying with her conviction even though it may be necessary to delay action until her child is a little more mature, constitutes a strong and positive sense of self. The backing and emotional support of the seething feminist movement appears to be cresting, and change is the hallmark of life today. Change subsumes choice, and here the horizons have indeed widened. Women are currently working in fields formerly closed to them by discrimination against women or some other form of restriction. The former vitriolic attacks on men as the "Oppressor" seem to have moderated and perhaps displaced onto the legislative approach, releasing a greater amount of positive energy for use in forging ahead. There are suggestions of relevant psycho-social dynamics, and modified versions of the therapeutic use of groups. These would seem to need systematic study, for they as well as other segments of the feminist rationale still lack a theoretical base. There are, however, gratifications from the group solidarity so obvious at the meetings, and some progress in self awareness, understanding, and esteem all so basic to self counseling. Another area which imperatively asks for further study are the intrapsychic interactions within the family, especially the children's response to mothers who work.

[221]

Among early teen-agers and even older girls, identity has a new meaning; it is called *doing one's thing*. Developmentally it seems propelled by a powerful bid for autonomy as well as an expression of the self-love phenomenon. Many girls around age 14 display an identity hunger; they do only such activities as they enjoy and avoid what they dislike — "anything boring." When their dedication involves school assignments and the students ignore them, school failure often follows. Few students enjoy the drill phases of learning, but they recognize its place in mastering a subject and are carried along by their absorption in their *thing*. At times this is shared by other students, usually cliques who are turned on, for instance, by new forms of music. But this makes for an uneven development of interpersonal relations so vital in identity building.

Currently there is an outcropping of experimental work along these lines with a special group of high school seniors, in a school setting where students plan the curriculum and assign classes. But I have been unable to find any report on it. Surely such a program offers positive values, promoting initiative, insight, and serves in setting sights toward occupational goals. In none of the discussions on this subject (and they have been limited) have I heard mention of the significance of the balance between "give and take" concept as an important step in development. It includes an awareness that one may need to compromise goals, to give as well as take, and meet the challenge of added responsibility.

This writer would like to see the emphasis on work life become more career oriented, replacing the current narrower focus on jobs. When women achieve a high degree of self-actualization through using their talents maximally, imaginatively, and meaningfully, they will grow as individuals and contribute to a society which is in dire need of their unique type of help.

## APPENDIX
### The Prediction Study

Can valid predictions be made about occupational choice in girls who are in the process of maturing from middle to late adolescence? Even if they are not verified by outcome, the process of prediction can be used as a research tool, a learning instrument, and as a means of validation and refinement of some of the concepts we have used — concepts such as identification pattern, relative resolution of phase specific tasks, and capacity to modify experience. We can learn both from our errors and our successes.

After the first contact with the high school seniors, predictions were made concerning changes to be expected in three years' time. The changes specified were those having to do with identification pattern, ego synthesis, the structure, nature, and direction of identity formation and occupational role as conceptualized in the theoretical framework of the study.

The same predictive statements were not made for all ten subjects of this study. Rather, the researchers, after the completion of the initial interviews with parents and subjects plus testing procedures, made for each subject a group of individualized predictions before the follow-up interview with the subject. These were considered tentative in nature, representing impressions taken from an organismic view of the subject and focused on developmental aspects. [With nine of the ten subjects, the predictions were done by Friend.]

The total number of predictions made for each subject ranged from 19 to 35, wtih an average of 27. To determine the accuracy of their outcome, two independent judges read the complete record of each girl including the follow-up interviews and the blind analyses of the psychological testing. Next they rated independently each prediction on a five-point scale following the scoring system of Escalona and Heider (1959) / (1-Correct, 2-Predominantly Correct, 3-Predominantly False, 4-False, and finally 5-Unknown.) The category of Unknown was used for items which the judges could not rate because of lack of outcome information or occasionally because the language of the predictive statement was ambiguous.

Both judges found that most ratings could be made clearly and quickly. Those which were most difficult were predictions whose outcome had to be inferred or interpreted from the existing data whether it was taken from psychological testing or interview reports, for example, the prediction "ambivalence toward the mother will diminish."

In comparing their ratings, the judges also followed the technique of Escalona and Heider (1959). When confronted with a discrepancy in their ratings, they first determined whether the prediction in question had been understood differently by each. Often the wording of the prediction yielded somewhat different meanings to the two readers. In the great majority of such cases the judges were able to come quickly to a consensus for meaning. There were other cases where a discrepancy in the rating arose not from the predictive statement itself but from disagreement over interpretation of the outcome material. In these cases the judges discussed the reasons behind their opinions in an attempt to reconcile the difference. It is interesting to note that none of the rating discrepancies remaining after such discussions involved a correct-false discrepancy. In other words, whenever the two judges disagreed, it was over the degree of correctness or the degree of falseness of any one prediction. The following table indicates for each subject the percentage of total agreement achieved by the judges. The ratings included in these percentages do not include those for which reconciliation had to be made.

[224]

*Percentage of total agreement between the two judges' scores*

| | |
|---|---|
| Pat * | 94% |
| Joy | 94% |
| Vi | 88% |
| Rachel | 88% |
| Lois | 87% |
| Meg | 86% |
| Ann | 85% |
| Kay | 83% |
| Enid | 75% |
| Emily | 75% |

Following their scoring, the data items were systematized into groupings which had already been derived from the theoretical grounding of the study. Predictions were thus separated into three classes: Identification Pattern; Ego Synthesis; and Structure, Nature, and Direction of Occupational Choice. After the predictions had all been rated and classified, procedures were carried out to determine what percentage of predictions were confirmed (success ratio).

When all the predictions had been rated (along with any necessary reconciliations between judges) and classified, and after incomplete outcome predictions were eliminated, 267 predictions remained. Their distribution is shown in the accompanying table:

*Distribution of the 267 outcome ratings*

| | | | |
|---|---|---|---|
| Correct | 131 | 49% | |
| Predominantly Correct | 72 | 28% | 77% |
| Predominantly False | 24 | 8% | |
| False | 14 | 5% | 23% |
| Outcome Unknown | 26 | 10% | |
| Total | 267 | 100% | |

---

*Pat is the only mid-adolescent subject reported fully here.

[225]

It seems clear that the great majority of predictions were upheld. The combined categories of Correct and Predominantly Correct ratings comprise 77 per cent of all the rated predictions better than five times the percentage of false or inaccurate predictions (categories of False and Predominantly False) were made only 13 per cent of the time. Ten per cent of the predictions were placed in the unknown or undetermined category.

The following table presents a breakdown of the predictions into the three classes or categories to which they were assigned.

*Distribution of the 267 outcome ratings by classification*

|  | Identification Pattern | | Occupational Structure, Nature, and Direction | | Ego Synthesis | |
|---|---|---|---|---|---|---|
| Correct | 57 | 47% | 33 | 49% | 40 | 50% |
| Predominantly Correct | 32 | 26% | 13 | 19% | 27 | 33% |
| Predominantly False | 15 | 13% | 3 | 6% | 6 | 8% |
| False | 6 | 6% | 5 | 7% | 3 | 3% |
| Unknown | 9 | 8% | 13 | 19% | 5 | 6% |

It appears that predictions about Identification Pattern are correctly made *more* frequently than those concerning Structure, Nature, and Direction of Occupational Identity which is a multidimensional concept. An even higher success ratio resulted on the *Ego Synthesis* items. The number of predictions is often too small in any one case to allow for *statistical* verification of their significance. By inspection alone, however, the success ratio is considerably better than chance; these data offer heuristic value.

The trends which appear can be theoretically understood. Predictions concerning ego synthesis revolve around changes in various ego status consisting predominantly of the mastering of experience and integration of identifications, consolidation, and of progress toward more mature ways of behaving. The classes of outcome behavior used in rating such predictions are those which more often than not include behavior directly observable, or from inferences made from interview or test responses. Conversely the kinds of predictions which proved most difficult to rate required judging from inferences already several steps away from behavioral data.

Another kind of difference between predictions which may affect success ratios concerns dimensionality. An unidimensional prediction, while on the one hand perhaps easier to rate, is also more simply judged correct or false. A prediction of multi-dimensions can be judged partially if not totally correct, thus still adding to the success ratio. These kinds of differences between predictions and their effects on possible success ratios were not systematically studied within the framework of this study. Such information would be of value to any professional person trying to find ways to make valid reliable predictions for young people and their occupational development. This applies especially to counselors who evaluate and predict silently throughout their working day.

A smaller accuracy in predicting characterizes the grouping called "Structure, Nature, and Direction" of occupational role. Nature refers to the kind of occupation chosen; while direction applies to whether or not the future life will feature family only (not working outside but concentrating on home and care of family); "double track" (family care combined with an occupation outside of the home). Either can be linked further with social activities, clubs, political activities, et cetera. Structure implies the degree of crystallization of a definitive role and involves the decision process as well as characteristic defenses. There were limitations to predicting "Nature" because some of the seniors had already decided this. In one instance, Joy, the switch of the subject's college majors from pre-medicine to art was correctly predicted, mostly on the basis of the Rorschach, and the creative temperament of the girl. So, too, with a girl who could not qualify for the profession of physical therapist. Some form of nursing was anticipated for Kay; she became a practical nurse, an occupation which had not been mentioned in the early interviews. In another girl, pursuit of dancing was predicted but also the need to fail. Although Vi did fail in her course in dancing, she may succeed in the actual practice of the art. In the meantime, at 24 she is carrying out mother's wishes by returning to college contrary to her own wishes.

An early or late marriage was difficult to predict with accuracy; the husband himself has considerable impact on future choices. Vi, who spoke disparagingly of marriage, actually took the step at 23. For Lois, whose interests fluctuated between research in chemistry, teaching, and medicine, we thought she would delay marriage for pursuit of profession but she was wed about six months after graduation. Her husband, however, is a doctor who helps her with her work in medical research. Although she still may study medicine, her husband feels that she will find it arduous.

So many forces vary at the same time in the lives of the girls that these processes impinge on accuracy of prediction. This accuracy can be improved when one is clearer about what lends itself to prediction and what does not; also to more of the general principles applying to the field. Currently success ratio favors ego synthesis and changes in identification pattern. The former deals more with the process of handling choice of an occupational role, whereas identifications often impel a choice.

The content of the predictions which did hold up were certainly consonant with some of the theory behind this study. To illustrate the kinds of predictions from each of the three classes most frequently borne out, a partial list follows. (A summary statement has been made in each case from the individual wordings of similar predictions.) It is interesting to note that the predictions uphold the formulation that the occupational identity is part and parcel of the total sense of self. As one of

[228]

the predictions actually states, the occupational role becomes delineated as the personal identity takes shape. To carry it further, identity formation and occupational role interpenetrate.

A. *Identification Patterns*
   1. Identification with mother will become more positive.
   2. Communication with father will improve.
   3. Teacher and career identification figures will increase in importance.
   4. Feminine identification will "firm."
   5. Expressions of real feelings, negative as well as positive, will increase.
   6. Peer group identifications will continue or increase.

B. *Structure, Nature and Direction of Occupational Goal*
   1. The occupational goal will become more directed, articulated. She will probably teach for a while.
   2. In the course of forming an occupational role, the present goal choice may change.

C. *Ego Synthesis*
   1. Methods of coping with problems will strengthen.
   2. As the personal identity takes shape, the occupational role will be delineated.

Although only a sample prediction is included in the Appendix, many others of real theoretical interest were made so infrequently that they do not lend themselves to any kind of grouping. We have placed before each prediction *one* asterisk to indicate correct or predominantly correct predictions, *two* asterisks for the false or predominantly false ones. One recommendation for future studies of this sort is that the scope of the predictive analysis be enlarged.

* * *

A word about how the predictions were made by the author. It was decided to focus the expectations on the same categories used in the life histories: family information, dynamics, and transactions among family members; identification pattern; ego

[229]

development according to the Erikson and Blos stages; school and college achievements; personality and teacher's evaluation; personality organization according to impressions of projective tests at two intervals three years apart; nature and direction of occupational role.

As an example, parents were evaluated on the basis of how they play their parts as identification figures. It seemed important to evaluate, for instance, the degree to which the mother accepted her role in life and possessed the flexibility to change with the child. Changes over time were expected, but we needed to delve beyond these. The predictor asked herself: how is she functioning now, in school, with friends and at home? Has she started to detach herself from the family? What are her attitudes toward herself and others? Are identity and occupational goal crystallizing? How realistically? How does she see her future? What was she like as an infant, and how did the feeding period go? Similarly what do we know of the journey through other stages? What were parental, play, and early work identifications like?

After rereading all of the material, the predictor made some tentative predictions working rather quickly. Then she found herself picturing the subject in a number of the above situations, became quite absorbed in the subject, even to the point of brooding. About a month later she revised the predictions, and stated in most instances the reasons for what she had anticipated. In some instances, she did not know the reason. But the revisions were based on a more systematic, analytic kind of thinking than the intuitive kind used in the first go-over. Even the second and third revisions were not quite as systematic as she would have liked them to be.

In giving evidence, she extrapolated from what knowledge she had of personality and identity development, paying particular attention to mechanisms of consolidation, integration, and synthesis. From time to time before the follow-up interview

[230]

which was the deadline for turning the predictions in, she made minor changes or added predictions. In most of the cases, the first tentative impressions were left unchanged. The process of prediction did not come easily; others may develop different ways of forecasting.

Because a high percentage of the predictions proved correct does not necessarily mean that it followed causally from the reason specified; rather some unknown factor may have been operating.

Which of the girls were we able to predict for with most and least success? At the apex was Pat, next Joy. Both revealed what seemed to be their real selves on both the projective tests and the interview data as well as in their actual behavior. Both have a higher degree of self awareness, and easier access to deeper levels of personality. In addition, the parents gave us a good deal of authentic information. All of this seemed to fall into a pattern. What else contributed we do not know. At the nadir of the ranking were Enid and Rachel. Enid's functioning is quite uneven; moverover, her parents push her a good deal to get a job, and have mixed feelings about what she should do. Her high anxiety takes the form of vacillation, and decisions depend on the person she talked to last. Indecision may be a revenge technique against her parents.

With Rachel, there was a wide discrepancy between what she communicated on tests and what she told us during the interview, also between the counselor's and the psychologist's impression of the parents.

The rest of the girls clustered quite closely near the top of the ranking: the range was not large. It may be that a predictor feels varying degrees of empathy for particular girls which affects the success ratio or that there is an effort to be consistent of which the predictor is not aware.

[In the appendix we have included a sample breakdown of the predictions for one girl.]

SYLVIA D. KORSTVEDT, PH.D.
ARNE S. KORSTVEDT, PH.D.

[231]

# BIBLIOGRAPHY
## Books and Articles Cited or Consulted

Allport, G. *Pattern and Growth in Personality.* New York: Holt, Reinhart & Winston, 1961.

Arbuckle, D. *Counseling and Psychotherapy: An Overview.* New York: McGraw Hill, 1967.

Bettelheim, B. *The Informed Heart.* New York: The Free Press, 1963.

Blaine, G. B., and McArthur, C. C. *Emotional Problems of the Student.* New York: Appleton-Century-Crofts, 1961.

Blos, P. *On Adolescence.* New York: The Free Press of Glencoe, 1962.

Borow, H., ed. *Man in a World at Work.* Boston: Houghton Mifflin, 1963.

Coles, R. *Erik H. Erikson: The Growth of His Work.* Boston: Atlantic-Little, Brown, 1970.

Deutsch, H. *Psychology of Women,* vol. 1. New York: Grune & Stratton, 1944.

Erikson, E. H. "Identity and the Life Cycle," *Psychological Issues,* vol. 1, No. 1, New York: International Universities Press, 1959.

———. *Childhood and Society.* New York: W. W. Norton, 1959. Second edition, 1963.

———. "The Golden Rule and the Cycle of Life," *Harvard Medical Alumni Bulletin,* Winter, 1963.

Escalona, S. and Heider, G. M. *Predictions and Outcome.* New York: Basic Books, 1959.

Friend, J. G., and Haggard, E. A. *Work Adjustment in Relation to Family Background.* Psychological Monograph No. 16. American Psychological Association. Stanford: Stanford Press, 1948.

Freud. A. *Normality and Pathology in Childhood.* New York: International Universities Press, 1965.

Ginzberg, E., *et al. Occupational Choice.* New York: Columbia University Press, 1965.

Hartman, H. E., and Loewenstein, C. R. *Notes on the Theory of Aggression-Psychic Structure in the Psychoanalytic Study of the Child.* New York: International Universities Press, 1946.

Holland, J. L. "Major Progress of Research on Vocational Behavior," in *Man in a World of Work*, H. Borow, ed. Boston: Houghton Mifflin, 1964.

Hollingshead and Redlich, "Personality Differences Between Middle and Upper Classes," *J. of Abnormal and Social Psychology*, vol. 50, 1955.

Inhelder, B., and Piaget, J. *The Growth of Logical Thinking*. New York: Basic Books, 1958.

Mathewson, R. H. *Guidance Policy and Practice*. 3rd edition. New York: Harper & Row, 1962.

Millet, Kate. *Sexual Politics*. New York: Doubleday, 1970.

Murray, H. A. *Explorations in Personality*. New York: Oxford University Press, 1938.

Murphy, L. *The Widening World of Childhood*. New York: Basic Books, 1962.

Nachman, B. "Childhood Experiences and Vocational Choice in Law, Dentistry and Social Work." *J. of Counseling Psychology*, 7:243, 1960.

Neff, W. *Work and Human Behavior*. New York: Atherton Press, 1969.

Parsons, T. *The Social System*. New York: The Free Press of Glencoe, 1951.

Roe, A. *The Psychology of Occupations*. New York: John W. Wiley, 1959.

——. "Early Determinants of Vocational Choice," *J. of Counseling Psychology*, 41:215, 1957.

Schafer, R. *Aspects of Internalization*. New York: International Universities Press, 1970.

Segal, S. J. "A Psychoanalysis of Personality Factors in Vocational Choice," *J. of Counseling Psychology*, 8:202, 1961.

Super, D. E. "The Psychology of Careers," in *Man in a World of Work*, H. Borow, ed. Boston: Houghton Mifflin, 1955.

Tiedeman, D. V. "Harvard Studies in Career Development," Cambridge: Harvard Graduate School of Education.

Tiedeman, D. V. and O'Hara, R. P. *Career Development: Choice and Adjustment*. New York: College Entrance Examination Board, 1963.

Van Hoose and Peietrofes. *Counseling and Guidance in the Twentieth Century*. Boston: Houghton Mifflin, 1970.

White, R. W., ed. *A Study of Lives: In Honor of H. A. Murray*. New York: Atherton Press, 1963.

White, R. W. *Lives in Progress.* New York: Henry Holt, 1960. Second Edition, 1966.

———. "Ego and Reality in Psychoanalytic Theory," *Psychological Issues,* vol. 3, no. 3, 1963.

———. "Motivation Reconsidered: The Concept of Competence," *Psychological Review,* vol. 66, 1959.

Winnecut, D. "Transitional Objects and Transitional Phenomena," *Int. J. of Psychoanalysis,* 34:89, 1953.

Yeo, J. W., and Billett, R. *Growing Up.* Boston: D. C. Heath, 1951.